Latin American Journey

LATIN
✠
AMERICAN
✠
JOURNEY
✠

*Insights for
Christian Education
in North America*

ROBERT W. PAZMIÑO

Wipf and Stock Publishers
EUGENE, OREGON

Wipf and Stock Publishers
199 West 8th Avenue, Suite 3
Eugene, Oregon 97401

Latin American Journey
Insights for Christian Education in North America
By Pazmiño, Robert W.
Copyright©1994 Pazmiño, Robert W.
ISBN: 1-59244-034-7
Publication date: September, 2002
Previously published by United Church Press, 1994.

To my son, David Bruce Pazmiño, who has studied the history of Latin America and my cousins and Christian sisters and brothers in Latin America.

Contents

Preface · **ix**

Introduction: An Incredible Journey · **xi**

1 · An Encounter with Liberation Theologies · **1**

2 · The Implications of Liberation Theology
for Education · **28**

3 · Transformative Christian Education · **55**

4 · Theological Education of the Whole People of God · **76**

5 · Multicultural Christian Education and Values
in Hispanic Culture · **106**

6 · Possibilities for the Future Journey Together · **123**

Notes · **147**

Bibliography · **159**

Index · **167**

Preface

This work emerged from a journey to Latin America in which I
learned to see the challenges of Christian education from a new
perspective. This journey enabled me, in my own outlook, to re-
verse the traditional flow of influence from North America to the
south as I endeavored to learn from what God is doing among the
people, churches, schools, and communities in Latin America. I
was able then to relate what I learned to the situation in North
America. This journey also afforded me a personal opportunity, as
a North American Hispanic, to explore my Latin roots by visiting
for the first time the land of my ancestors' origin.

The introduction to this work recounts some of the particulars of
this incredible journey through the countries of Costa Rica, Ecuador, and Nicaragua. The focus will be upon the personal significance of the journey. Chapter 1 presents the unique challenges
posed by liberation theologies for the ongoing life and work of the
Christian church throughout the Americas, both North and South.
It also considers a reappraisal of this theological perspective which
has elicited both positive and negative reactions globally. Chapter 2
explores the implications of liberation theology for religious and
theological education, with special reference to the pioneering
work of the Brazilian educator Paulo Freire. Chapter 3 presents a
model of Christian education based on what can be learned from an
analysis of God's mission in the world and the place of Christian
education in relation to that mission. This model draws upon what
was learned from Latin American developments. One of these

developments, the rise of theological education for the whole people of God, is the focus of chapter 4, along with a comparison of the conflict and equilibrium paradigms for education, which serve to distinguish Latin American and North American concerns. Chapter 5 discusses in detail the model of multicultural education and highlights the values of Hispanic culture as one contributing partner to the multicultural feast that is now possible on a global scale. The final chapter, chapter 6, makes a number of suggestions for the future of Christian education through the consideration of the themes of partnership, potentials, and problems as they relate to the task of rebuilding Christian education. What was learned from my journey south has provocative implications for the task of rebuilding in the years ahead.

I am grateful to a host of persons and communities who welcomed and supported both me and my family during our time in Latin America. Special appreciation is due to the families of the *Desamparados* community and the students, faculty, and staff of the Latin American Biblical Seminary in San José, Costa Rica. In addition, the members of the Emaús Christian community must be remembered for their gracious care and support through the difficult times of our initial adjustment as strangers in a new land. Finally, special thanks is offered to my loving extended family in Ecuador, who welcomed a distant cousin and his family from the United States with open arms.

It was not an easy task returning to New England as a North American Hispanic following our time in Latin America. The challenge of that return I trust will be obvious to the reader after reading chapter 5 of this work. But return I did, and I offer my reflections to the North American Christian community of which I am a member.

Introduction:
An Incredible Journey

At the age of twelve, Jesus took an incredible journey with his parents to Jerusalem, a journey described for us in Luke 2:41–51:

> Now every year his parents went to Jerusalem for the festival of the Passover. And when he was twelve years old, they went up as usual for the festival. When the festival was ended and they started to return, the boy Jesus stayed behind in Jerusalem, but his parents did not know it. Assuming that he was in the group of travelers, they went a day's journey. Then they started to look for him among their relatives and friends. When they did not find him, they returned to Jerusalem to search for him. After three days they found him in the temple, sitting among the teachers, listening to them and asking them questions. And all who heard him were amazed at his understanding and his answers. When his parents saw him they were astonished; and his mother said to him, "Child, why have treated us like this? Look, your father and I have been searching for you in great anxiety." He said to them, "Why were you searching for me? Did you not know that I must be in my Father's house?" But they did not understand what he said to them. Then he went down with them and came to Nazareth, and was obedient to them. His mother treasured all these things in her heart.

The distance Jesus and his parents traveled from Nazareth to Jerusalem, about seventy-five miles, usually required five days on foot. As might be expected on so long and arduous a journey, something unanticipated occurred: Jesus stayed behind and his parents left Jerusalem, assuming that he was in their company. Parents today can imagine the anxiety Mary and Joseph experienced in returning and searching for their son throughout the city.

Modern travelers may be able to identify readily with the various experiences of Jesus and his parents—sharing similar experiences of excitement, anxiety, and delight that characterize some journeys as "incredible." This was my experience on a journey that brought my family and me from New England to Latin America.

As an educator reflecting on this account from the Gospel of Luke, I am fascinated with how Jesus is described as sitting among the teachers in the Temple courts. A pattern can be discerned here in Jesus' interaction with the teachers, which is repeated in Luke 24:13–35. In this later narrative, Jesus interacts with two disciples journeying with him on the road to Emmaus. The pattern of Jesus' learning in the Temple and his teaching of the disciples later in life was threefold: Jesus listened to what others were saying; he raised questions for the teachers in the Temple and the disciples on the road; and he shared his understanding and answers. Effective education occurs when people listen actively and sensitively, raise questions based upon what they hear and discern, and share with integrity, as a gift to others, the wisdom they have gained. Such education assumes interpersonal interaction and a willingness to dialogue.

It is my intent in this work to share with you, the readers, an account of an incredible journey not unlike the one the twelve-year-old Jesus experienced in Jerusalem. I will share what I learned in Latin America through listening and raising questions, especially any wisdom I may have gained in addressing the challenges of religious education in the United States. So much can be learned through dialogue with our sisters and brothers who live south of our border. Such an exchange of ideas is particularly crucial at this time when a commitment to globalization in our world necessitates an effective sharing of resources between North and South in the

Americas to complement our historical and current fascination with East-West developments. This fascination can be partly understood by the traditional reading of U.S. history, which sees the progress of the nation as a movement from the East Coast to the West Coast. This all-too-typical perspective does not recognize developments prior to the Pilgrims' arrival in New England, which involved Spanish settlement in what is now the southern region of the nation.[1] But that represents another story; and at this point, it is necessary to share selective and memorable aspects of my travels as they affected me.

Where Did I Go?

My eight-month journey, between September 1988 and May 1989, was spent primarily in the Central American republic of Costa Rica. I was exploring alternative forms of theological and religious education in Latin America in the hope of learning about new ways to address the needs of increasingly diverse multicultural communities in the United States. I lived with my wife and five-year-old daughter in San José, the capital of Costa Rica, in an urban area called *"Los Desamparados,"* which translated from Spanish means "those abandoned or forsaken." Though there were times when I felt at a loss and somewhat abandoned in a new culture with my first immersion experience abroad, I, as a North American Hispanic, welcomed the unique opportunity to be in Latin America and to explore my roots. For people from ethnic- or cultural-minority communities, this exploration of roots serves to ground one's identity and to connect with an all-too-readily forgotten past. My exploration included the countries of Costa Rica, Ecuador, and Nicaragua.

Costa Rica

Costa Rica, which was our home away from home, is a country of about 3.2 million persons, living within an area of twenty thousand square miles—roughly the size of West Virginia, or from a New England perspective, New Hampshire and Vermont combined. It is bordered on the north by Nicaragua and on the south by

Panama, two nations that historically have experienced U.S. intervention in their internal affairs. As a nation, Costa Rica has been popularized as an oasis of peace and relative tranquility in a very troubled region of the world. Given its location and commitment to peaceful economic and political growth, Costa Rica has become home to refugees from the North and South, including over twenty thousand North Americans who may be described as refugees from the income tax that diminishes their retirement income. In 1984, Costa Rica declared its perpetual unarmed neutrality; and it has had no standing army since 1949, when its then President José (Pepe) Figueres abolished the military following a civil war. I was intrigued to learn about education in such a setting, surrounded by the larger regional conflicts engulfing Central America.

As a nation, Costa Rica spends a major portion of its national budget on social welfare programs such as health, housing, and education. In regard to housing, one Costa Rican pastor, Jorge Gaitán, who visited our home following our return to the States, was appropriately appalled to learn that a nation as rich as the United States has so many homeless people. This is not the case in Costa Rica. In 1989, Costa Rica spent $200 million on education alone, or 23.5 percent of its budget, honoring its commitment to provide free public education from kindergarten to the twelfth grade, along with an extensive network of nearly twenty universities, technical colleges, and extension programs for those who must work. Such a commitment is noteworthy given the high percentage of the population who are children and youths. Extensive national support for higher education makes it possible for the most able students to complete their college education regardless of financial ability. The example of such a commitment may be an encouragement to the continuing national discussion regarding education in the United States. A strong national commitment to education in more than just words and political posturing was noteworthy.

In its recent history as a nation, Costa Rica has confronted five major problems that have significance on a global scale. The first major problem confronting Costa Rica is the external debt, as is the case in most Latin America countries. In the United States, the public also has struggled with its national debt in the effort not to live off the earnings of future generations. In Costa Rica, this problem is first in terms of its magnitude and impact. The debt is a political problem as well as an economic one because it obviously affects the standard of living and the peace and well-being of more than 350 million persons throughout Latin America, as well as the viability of democratic progress at both the national and international levels.

A second major problem is rapid population growth because family-planning rights are not fully realized, with teenage pregnancy representing about 20 percent of the annual births. This population growth adds increased demands upon limited resources, and teenage births impair the economic viability of young families. In the United States, the rise of teenage pregnancy has posed a similar challenge.

A third problem of significant impact is extensive deforestation, with Costa Rica ranking as one of the world's worst nations in this regard. Many forests have been cleared to provide grazing land for cattle, which in turn have been sold to the United States, satisfying the high demands for beef consumption. One must also note the impact upon every nation of the global ecological crisis, an increasingly important factor in U.S. policy decisions.

The fourth problem, exacerbated by deforestation, is environmental pollution from both industrial and domestic wastes. This problem is complicated by the continued sale of agricultural products banned in other Western nations because of their toxicity and environmental impact but sold extensively for use in Latin America.[2] Although much of the produce grown with such chemicals is in turn exported to the United States, this situation has greater health impacts upon local populations in Central America than abroad.

The fifth primary problem confronting this Central American nation is that of inflation, which rises at a 15 to 20 percent annual rate. My family and I observed a dramatic rise in the cost of milk and other food products, electricity, and water during our stay without any corresponding rise in the wages of Costa Rican workers. In 1989, it was estimated that 74 percent of the population was living below the poverty line, without enough money even to purchase the *canasta basica*—the basic market basket of food products. This results in the majority of people eating poorly, with long-term effects in relation to national progress and economic productivity. The impact of undernourishment is devastating wherever poverty is experienced throughout the Americas. In the United States, those on fixed incomes are the ones most affected by inflationary trends.

These five problems took on personal dimensions as a result of our living with the people in a local Costa Rican community. I was better able to recognize these problems and their manifestations in the United States by being in a totally new setting. In Costa Rica, my family and I lived on one block of a neighborhood constituting a small, closely knit community of twenty-five working- and middle-class families that included fifty children. Needless to say, my extroverted five-year-old daughter was delighted with all the friends at our doorstep. With a large portion of the population consisting of children and youths, this nation has very wisely stressed education and health needs in planning for its future. We were the only North Americans living in the area, so initially we were greeted as novelties. We lived in the home of the Araya family, who, like us, were experiencing a sabbatical year abroad, which brought them from their home in Costa Rica to Canada. As strangers, we were warmly welcomed and supported by our neighbors throughout our stay.

Ecuador

In addition to our time in Costa Rica, for three weeks in January 1989 we visited Ecuador, a small South American country located on the equator, from which its name derives. The "we" at this point included my mother-in-law, who arrived in January and shared our Latin American venture for three months. She was doing research for her social-work position with the public elementary school system of New York City, investigating the social services available to school children. My wife was working part time as a recruiter for a small women's college in Massachusetts, which required her to visit private high schools. Thus, with my mother-in-law's visits to elementary schools, my wife's visits to secondary schools, and my visits to schools of higher education and programs for adults, we covered the whole gamut of schooling efforts across the age span.

The lasting value for me of this journey was the opportunity to share it with my immediate and extended family. This particular leg of my trip held special personal significance, in that my great-grandparents and grandparents came to the United States from Ecuador in 1900, settling in New York City. The visit to Ecuador provided a unique opportunity to meet family members for the first time and to explore the Latin roots of my extended family.

Ecuador is a democratic republic of 10.6 million persons, with an area about the size of Colorado. Unlike Costa Rica's population, of which only 3 percent is of African heritage and 1 percent is indigenous, 25 percent of Ecuador's population consists of indigenous peoples and 10 percent of people of African heritage. This cultural diversity reminded us of the cosmopolitan urban atmosphere of New York City. As a nation, Ecuador has struggled with the problems of illiteracy, malnutrition, and infant mortality. In addition, the effects of inflation and a burdensome external debt have seriously limited reform efforts.

One aspect of life that impressed us was the vast gap between the rich and poor in Ecuador, but we later realized that it was not unlike the widening income gap that exists in the United States. I was particularly aware of this situation while in Ecuador because some members of my family belong to the upper economic class and have a number of servants in their home. The distinct nature of our interactions with these servants, treating them as persons as well as workers, occasioned conversations regarding our views and perspectives. In addition, we were the first Protestants—known in Latin America as *evangelicos* or "evangelicals" regardless of one's theological perspective—to be entertained in the homes of my family, providing a basis for theological discussion. But with all of our differences, we established strong and lasting ties on this brief trip, which at my Ecuadorian family's insistence was extended a week beyond our original plans. Many tears were shed at our departure, with a longing on the part of my immediate family to return, God willing, in the days ahead.

As one direct result of this time in Ecuador, my wife and I were able to serve as surrogate parents for my cousin's son, who upon our return to the States came from Ecuador for one year to study in a nearby boarding school in Massachusetts. The ties that can link people across national and cultural borders are characteristic of the emerging multicultural and global society that increases the occurrence of what can be called "crossover experiences."

My journey from North to Central and South America was personally and symbolically a crossing over, just as the Israelites crossed over both the Red Sea and the Jordan River. Throughout the biblical record, one hears of people crossing over and gaining new insights. Elisha crossed over the river and was empowered to address new challenges of ministry following the departure of Elijah (2 Kings 2:7–14). This was symbolized in Elisha's receiving Elijah's mantle. The good Samaritan crossed over to the other side of the road to encounter the wounded traveler and was recognized by Jesus and perhaps later by Paul as being a true Jew of the heart (Rom. 2:28–29). I crossed for the first time in my life to Latin America and there encountered people and realities new to me, which helped me to better understand what I left at home. In crossing over, I was exploring the roots of my ancestors who left the country of Ecuador to find a new life in the United States. The departure of my family from Ecuador was related to the earlier excommunication of my great-grandfather from the Roman Catholic church for his political and journalistic activities. The exploration of his history was one highlight of my journey, giving depth and meaning to my ministry in unanticipated ways. I recognized the potential complicity the Christian church and I myself might be subject to in resisting God's work in the world as evidenced in this history.

My great-grandfather, Felicísimo López, was a physician and politician during the presidency of General Eloy Alfaro, who served two terms as president of Ecuador from 1895 to 1901 and from 1906 to 1911.[3] During Alfaro's first term in office, Felicísimo López served as the Minister of *Fomento*, which included oversight of education and interior affairs. In Ecuadorian history, 1895 is known as the Year of the Revolution, with significant change occurring at various levels of society. Alfaro was known as a progressive or liberal politician who implemented policies to improve the living conditions of the indigenous peoples, who until then were little more than slaves. By executive order, he freed them from the forced labor they were periodically required to perform. The Roman Catholic church at that time opposed the liberal policies of the Alfaro government, which also worked for the separation of church and state. The historical context of my great-grandfather's ministry was fascinating to me as I considered the challenges I face as a North American Hispanic educator in the United States.

At the end of the nineteenth century, General Eloy Alfaro had emerged from the business classes as a leader of coastal reaction to Sierra conservatism and clericalism that dominated the nation of Ecuador. Those in political power in the Sierra were the landowning elite who were backed by the church and who supported the status quo. The emerging coastal liberal leadership supported new forms of capitalism and government. The anticlerical liberals, who included my ancestor, gradually removed the church from state education. They instituted civil marriage and burial, proclaimed freedom of religion, permitted divorce, and eased controls on the press. The church's imposed tithe was abolished, and many of its large estates were confiscated by the state, some passing into the hands of the liberal leaders themselves. The central government did not lose its authoritative caste with the liberal reforms of this time. Alfaro, the liberal political boss (*caudillo*), was as arbitrary and ruthless as his earlier conservative predecessor, President Gabriel García Moreno, whose history is itself enlightening.

García Moreno had concluded earlier in his life that the only social cement for society was religion, which for him meant the general adherence throughout the nation to the Roman Catholic church and its leadership. He emphasized strong personal rule and the central role of the church. All education and much government oversight was turned over to the clerics during the presidency of García Moreno, which included the terms of 1859–1861, 1861–1865, and 1869–1875. García Moreno was assassinated in 1875, but his political conservatism persisted in Ecuador until Alfaro's presidency, which came as a result of a national revolution. Following Moreno's organizational efforts under the auspices of the church in Ecuador, Alfaro's policies sought to dislodge the place of the church in society as a central political power.

The historical struggle as described here between liberal and conservative politics and policies continues in Ecuador and other Latin American nations today. On one visit to the Catholic university to arrange a visit with Father Miguel Ramos, an innovative theological educator and church leader, I identified myself as a descendent of Felicísimo López to Father Ramos's sister, who immediately described my forebear as being *"muy rojo,"* which means "very red." By this she meant that he was a radical socialist in his political stance. In reading Felicísimo's reflections—written in 1906, six years after his departure from Ecuador—I discovered that he did, in fact, espouse democratic and socialist ideals. These ideals included human rights for all people regardless of their ethnic origin.

The political, economic, social, and ideological divisions reflected in the general and familial history I explored during my visit to Ecuador present a continuing challenge to the wider church of Jesus Christ. What political position should the church advocate in the wider society? In Latin America, a stance of political neutrality is viewed as implicitly supporting the status quo, which may well be perpetuating gross injustices and human rights violations among the vast majority of people and communities. Latin America has been a center for the consideration of the political dimensions of theology and, in particular, the liberation theologies that will be explored in chapter 1.

As an educator, I was interested in how political arrangements affect the thought and practice of education. Alfaro's principal contribution to the field of education was in the systematic secularization of public education. His policies were not designed to suppress church schools, but rather to create state schools under lay control in accordance with the national need for an educated populace. Previously, educational opportunities had been very limited. Alfaro started the first night secondary school to address the need for an educated working class as a stable base for liberal progressive government. Although Alfaro opposed a theocratic government, he was not antireligious. This is important to note in relation to debates in the United States regarding the place of religion in public and private education. He stressed *mestizo* values of increased opportunities for all people, especially in terms of access to education. Alfaro's politics encouraged the organization of special instructional programs that permitted the urban working class to complete secondary school and to learn the essentials for a career while being gainfully employed. Alfaro consistently fostered policies designed to give women a more important role in government affairs. The revolution of 1895 thus ushered in an effort to popularize education in terms of its access and focus. The exploration of alternative forms of education has been a concern throughout the history of Latin America and the United States and Alfaro's administrations emphasized the popularization of education that has been a hallmark of public education in the United States.[4]

Prior to Alfaro's first presidential term, my great-grandfather was in conflict with clerics on political and educational issues and publicly expressed in the press his differences with the church. His stance resulted in his excommunication and the de facto ostracism of both him and his family from some levels of Ecuadorian society. This experience and others eventually lead the family to seek a new life in the United States. They arrived in New York City in 1900 with a diplomatic career arranged for Felicísimo López with the Alfaro government. My great-grandfather was attracted to the United States because of its commitments to public education and a democratic society.

Today, as in 1900, taking a stand in Latin America for justice and human rights can too readily result in exile or death, often not only for oneself but for one's family as well. I gained a new appreciation of the costs of working for social justice both in South and North America. My visit to Nicaragua provided an additional but brief glimpse into one nation's effort to realize a more just society in the wake of the historical tyranny of the Somoza regime.

Nicaragua

The third major stop on my journey was Nicaragua. In April 1989, I traveled for eight hours by van from San José, Costa Rica, to Managua, the capital, located in the western portion of the country. Nicaragua has a population of about 4.1 million people and an area about the size of Michigan, Iowa, or Georgia. At the time of my visit, the nation was under the Sandinista regime and was the continued target of United States opposition, which, along with mismanagement, had effectively devastated the economy. Nicaragua, on one hand, was maligned by the press in both the United States and Costa Rica and, on the other hand, was romanticized by those who supported a socialist or radical revolution in Latin America in order to improve the lot of the poor.

My perspective on the realities I observed in my limited exposure was somewhere between those two extremes. The Sandinistas appeared to be better revolutionaries than they were administrators of various sectors of the nation. One pastor aptly described the situation in the spring of 1989 this way: "The Contras had lost the war, but the Sandinistas had lost the economy." Many people were surviving through the informal economy, a network of goods and exchange that required people to work at second and third jobs just in order to survive and provide for their families. Since 1979 when the Sandinistas came to power, eight thousand professionals and technicians had left the country, constituting a major drain of people crucial for the support and progress of a struggling nation. The Sandinistas had made significant progress in addressing the survival needs of the poor, but the general decline of the nation and the tremendous outlay of resources for the Contra war set severe limitations.

As I walked the length of Managua and pondered the situation in the country on one hot Sunday afternoon in April 1989, I could not keep from wondering what was being accomplished by my nation's policies and extensive outlay of resources designed to bring this country to its knees economically and politically, at tremendous social cost. Ideological differences between the two nations were apparent, but the toll in human suffering was high. My thoughts returned to the group of Christian university students with whom I had shared an outing the day before, some with young families. What was the legacy being left for them, and how were my tax dollars being used to support their future? I had the privilege of hearing their dreams of a better life for their nation and their expressions of faith. I had seen their commitment to serve God and their people and had the privilege of encouraging them as we swam, picnicked, and talked together outside the capital city. I was sobered, heartened, and challenged. I thought again of the vast gap between the rich and the poor as I remembered my breakfast that morning at the exclusive downtown hotel and my lunch at the crowded eastern market where tourists do not visit. In my thoughts was the account of my companion at worship and at lunch that day, a pastor from the East Coast whose people had not experienced the benefits of the revolution and who was advocating for their human rights. What did the gospel have to say to all these people and to their situations? How could the body of Christ, the church, respond faithfully in this revolutionary situation? As a citizen of the United States, I had benefited from a revolution fought in the eighteenth century, and yet my government was effectively squelching a different kind of revolution in Nicaragua. These questions and thoughts were present for me during my time in this Central American republic and still remain with me in the recounting of my travels. As I struggled with these and other questions, my journey took on a unique character as a result of the company of traveling companions.

With Whom Did I Go?

Like Jesus, I shared this incredible journey with my family. As a spouse and parent with various responsibilities, my experience was vastly different from that of a twelve-year-old boy. But the opportunity to visit Latin America, and especially Ecuador, filled me with a joy reminiscent of boyhood pleasures and the anxieties of preadolescent adjustments. The opportunity of visiting new places and meeting new people with my family added a refreshing sense of adventure to the professional demands of seminary teaching and research. My wife's fluency in Spanish and my daughter's superior language-acquisition abilities meant that I, as a professor, would often have to profess my ignorance and graciously accept needed correction of my pronunciation of Spanish words. My daughter's

Costa Rican accent in speaking Spanish was perfect, and I re-learned the need to take risks in order to improve my own. I experienced the challenges of communicating in a second language as an adult and appreciated the support of interdependence a family can provide during times of transition. My family also provided an emotionally supportive setting in which to make sense of what at times was a frustrating maze of new systems to learn and contend with in a new culture. I was reminded of the importance of family support that is not the privilege of everyone today.

As a spouse and parent, I was required to plan this journey carefully, so as to anticipate as much as possible the various needs of my family while still allowing for the necessary flexibility to address unanticipated events along our way. Required were a good deal of advanced communication and a willingness to make contacts with people who initially were strangers but soon became close friends. The hospitality offered to us as strangers was remarkable. I was reminded again of the ability of children to develop relationships in much less time than is the case with adults. During my daughter's first day in kindergarten, she was invited to attend the birthday party of a classmate that very afternoon, linking our family with a number of other families at her school. The children of our neighborhood also organized a birthday party for my daughter a few weeks after our arrival. These were unique gifts to us as strangers in a new land.

One major unanticipated event during the first two weeks of our stay in Costa Rica was an automobile accident in which I was involved. Although I was not responsible for causing the accident, the only witness blamed me, and I was criminally charged and subject to possible imprisonment. After six months and a trying ordeal for the family, the case was heard in court; I was found guilty and sentenced to either pay a fifty-five-dollar fine or spend fifteen days in jail. I was tempted to accept the jail sentence to be able to write an account of a Central American prison, but at my wife's insistence and with better judgment, I paid the fine.

Through this experience, my family and I came to understand the value of having the support of our neighbors and of a Christian community. In addition, we were challenged to grow in our faith during this trial. I learned that Costa Rica has the second highest per capita accident rate in the world; and, by sharing the account of my accident, I had an immediate connection with a number of other persons in the community who had suffered similar mishaps. One of my neighbors later observed that the accident had enabled me to converse with a number of people and practice my Spanish conversation skills. I even met another professor, also on sabbatical in Costa Rica, who had had three accidents in the first month of his stay. I counted myself blessed to have only had only one. In addition, just three weeks prior to our return to the States, I was on the road to my daughter's school one morning when I encountered a family who had just been in an auto accident. This family befriended us, and I was pleased to be able to help provide them with transportation and to assist the husband with the bureaucratic procedures required to process the accident—procedures I had learned well from my earlier experience.

Through this and other experiences, I gained a renewed perspective of another traveling companion who accompanied us. Biblical teaching with regard to life and its journey reminds us of Abraham and Sarah, forebears of our faith, who with their household set out not knowing where they were going. We did know where we were going, but dealing with unanticipated events such as my auto accident raised questions about the nature of our journey. Abraham and Sarah encountered a number of difficulties and yet they were able to journey with some sense of peace and serenity. How was this possible for me and my family? Though Abraham and Sarah went out not knowing where they were going, they did know *with whom* they went. They were not alone, and there was one who assured them that they would not be forsaken and abandoned. Though they were uncertain as to the events they would encounter and the problems that would arise, they experienced the living God as their traveling companion. Similarly, my family and I were not abandoned in *Los Desamparados* (those forsaken), and we knew with whom we were traveling. This affirmation did not represent a mere veneer of faith over the trying experience of being a stranger in a strange land. Rather, it was an awareness of God's presence in the midst of a crisis, which provided the encouragement to travel on with the support of others. But what of those who are strangers and refugees across the globe? How are their experiences different from mine in the light of the biblical injunction to welcome the stranger and pilgrim in the land? Strangers we encounter in our homeland are present for a wide variety of reasons. Reflecting upon their experience as compared with mine helped me to gain perspective as I considered the motivations behind my journey south.

Why Did I Go?

As with any journey, I can name a variety of motives that lead to and guided my time in Latin America. Foremost in my concerns as a North American Hispanic, I wanted to be immersed in a Latin American context and to listen to what my Christian sisters and brothers were experiencing and saying. It was through the encouragement of the former dean of Andover Newton Theological School, Orlando Costas, that I first considered spending time in Costa Rica. Orlando and his family had spent ten years in Costa Rica as North American Hispanic missionaries. Orlando was one of the founders of the Latin American Evangelical Center for Pastoral Studies (CELEP), and he had served as the dean of the Latin American Biblical Seminary (SBL). With the death of Orlando in November 1987, my trip took on increased personal significance for me because I had been the first faculty member recruited and appointed during his tenure as dean. Orlando was the first Hispanic to serve as the academic dean in a major Protestant seminary in the United States. It was my privilege to teach in Spanish at the Latin American Biblical Seminary in February and March of 1989 and to closely observe the work of CELEP. Certainly the study and use of the Spanish itself was a second motive for my time in Costa Rica. Being bilingual as well as bicultural is essential in serving the North American Hispanic community in the United States.

My attraction to Central America must also be attributed to the interest that this region was receiving from the United States. Central America was viewed, and may still be viewed as a troubled area of the globe, caught up in the struggle between distinct ideologies and conceptions of human life. Central America has also been an area confronting both "high- and low-intensity war" and struggling with the search for peace. This search received global recognition in 1987 with the award of the Nobel Peace Prize to Oscar Arias, the former president of Costa Rica. The Latin American Biblical Seminary was also known as a center for the advocacy of liberation theologies, which have emerged in response to the conditions confronted by Christians throughout Central and South America. Studying and teaching at this school afforded a front-line view of some of the issues and tensions in the life of the church in Latin America, especially in relation to the development of alternative forms of theological education.

The focus of my research was the emergence of alternative forms of theological education in the context of Latin America. I have long had an interest in the work of renewal, reform, and transformation in education. The challenges posed for the church of Jesus Christ in Latin America required the exploration of alternatives to best serve the needs of various persons, many of whom did not have the luxury to take time away from their communities to experience residential study where education was being offered. I was curious to explore first-hand the new developments in theological education and to see what God was doing in the lives and ministries of my sisters and brothers in Central and South America. My personal encounter with a wide variety of people made my journey a life-changing experience. Those with whom I met contributed much to my learning.

Whom Did I Meet?

It was my privilege to meet an amazing variety of people in my immediate and surrounding communities, especially those associated with the Christian church in its various expressions. One impression I had in interacting with Latin American people was the extent to which some were divided from others in relation to their life orientation and a host of variables, including social class, race, gender, economic standing, political and ideological commitments, and church affiliation. In the churches, the divisions that exist in North America were duplicated in Latin America and complicated by divisions that represented timely indigenous and autonomous developments beyond foreign control. Persons who were historical contemporaries of these divisions were less open to work for reconciliation, the task of reconciliation being seen as a challenge for succeeding generations who were open to its possibility.

On a distinctly more hopeful note, I met a number of younger church leaders who were interested in facilitating dialogue among people from opposing camps. A fundamentalism of the right and the left could be identified in a number of contexts, with advocates of a mediating and balanced position within the existent and historical polarities being few and often misunderstood. One example of this situation emerged from my being affiliated with the Latin American Biblical Seminary, which has been associated with a radical and progressive stand that has affirmed the emergence of liberation theology and advocacy for the poor. As a result of this affiliation, a former student of mine who was teaching at the School of Pastoral Studies (ESEPA), an alternative seminary established as a result of the perceived heresy at SBL, informed me that I could not be asked to speak at ESEPA. It was assumed that I was guilty by association with SBL, given the emphasis upon the need to take sides in the battles of ecclesial politics. The embracing of liberation theologies at SBL resulted in the disassociation of a number of local churches from the support of the seminary and a distrust of that school's graduates.

In Costa Rica, I had the privilege of meeting a number of the faculty and students at SBL, who graciously welcomed and shared with me. They patiently encouraged my emerging Spanish-speaking abilities. Along with Janet May, a faculty member at SBL, I had the opportunity of teaching a course with five students: two Costa Rican women, both single parents, who were preparing for ordination; a young Costa Rican man interested in media education; a Nicaraguan woman who was recently married and settled in the area; and a Mexican pastor who had just arrived with his young family for the opportunity of further formal seminary study.

In the *Los Desamparados* community, my family and I met a warm and supportive group of individuals and families who provided support and advice to the *gringos*, the North Americans, who had arrived and needed help. We were welcomed as members of their families, and we shared in the joys and struggles of daily life. Our affiliation with a house church ministry that was emerging into a small congregation became our home ecclesial base as we visited a number of congregations during our stay. This house church, or base Christian community for the middle and professional class, began as an alternative to the institutional church and was modeled after an extended family of faith that embraced a wide variety of people including artists, teachers, leaders of parachurch organizations, professors, missionaries, and their families. The style of worship was informal and participatory, with both female and male leadership. Each Sunday service was followed by a common meal at which all were welcome, and the group frequently held additional social gatherings on other days of the week. The congregation surprised us at our home with an evening serenade of guitar music and traditional songs two nights before our return to United States. This group, who had welcomed us as strangers, sent us off from Costa Rica as close friends and members of the Emmaus Christian community.

From my journey I learned again of the importance of relationships in life and ministry. I gained a greater sense of personal identity through exploring my Ecuadorian roots and meeting family members for the first time, but also a greater sense of a shared humanity with other people from diverse backgrounds—Costa Ricans, Nicaraguans, and a host of persons from diverse national backgrounds brought together in a common human community. I believe the recovery and enhancement of this common humanity is a crucial task for the Christian church and one that calls for ecumenical and interfaith dialogue.

By rubbing shoulders and sharing my life and my family with people from different backgrounds, I was blessed with the insights and gifts they were able to share. In addition to our Costa Rican neighbors who warmly welcomed and supported us throughout our stay, my family and I interacted with an amazing host of folks. I team-taught with Janet May, a United Methodist missionary, originally from Iowa, who had studied in Texas and served with her family for nine years in Bolivia. Janet had much to teach me about

Christian education in Central America. We also became friends with a Brazilian family who had three children and who had recently arrived for three years of service in Costa Rica. This family represented three different denominations, which is itself a unique model for ecumenical cooperation. We also met a family with roots from Spain and Colombia who were serving with the United Nations in the area of refugee resettlement and who were no longer welcome in Costa Rica because of a disclosure they had made of misappropriation of funds by Costa Rican officials. In the house church, we shared special times with a missionary family in which the husband, like myself, was of Spanish and North American heritage and the wife of Dutch heritage from Michigan. Another family, the wife from Costa Rica and the husband from the Yucatán Peninsula of Mexico, was serving with the United Bible Societies. They were the leaders of the house church and supported us in many practical ways during our stay, including providing letters of reference to help us open a bank account—a chore that required two full days of effort. All of these relationships knit us together into a community, a network of persons who cared for and supported one another in time of need. Although we were strangers, this network provided us with a home away from home in a strange land that was rapidly losing its strangeness with each passing day.

Conclusion

In conclusion, this incredible journey meant a reaffirmation of the common humanity that we share with a host of people beyond our borders. It also strengthened my understanding of the unique ties that bind the Christian community, making Christ's reign a reality in this troubled world—a world desperately searching for peace with justice and the love of God that stands in relation to the truth of the gospel. But as was true of the twelve-year-old Jesus, much more lay ahead and much yet remains to be said about this journey and the greater journey of life with God that challenges each of us in our personal and corporate faith. One particular challenge that was posed for me was an encounter with liberation theologies in Latin America, which is the focus of chapter 1. This encounter represents a necessary alternative to the avoidance of dialogue between us, largely the privileged of North America, and our Latin American sisters and brothers with whom we share a common humanity. Exploring the contours of that common humanity along with the characteristics of the Christian community in its work on behalf of humanity is a distinct challenge for the ministries of Christian education at the close of the twentieth century. Such educational ministries are not solely the province of clergy but of the whole people of God, with their global connections and interdependencies, as I was able to see in my incredible Latin American journey.

An Encounter with
Liberation Theologies

Since the mid-1960s a new paradigm for theology has emerged in
Latin America with a corresponding sense of ferment and change.
This paradigm represents a new configuration of interests and concerns that moves away from the dominant image of equilibrium in
society to the image of change and conflict. Conflicts have been
experienced by the peoples of Latin America in the areas of political, economic, social, cultural, ideological, and religious life. But
at its most basic level, conflict in Latin America can be seen as the
conflict between life and death for many who daily struggle for
survival. At this basic level, the naming of realities confronting
Latin American society is a preliminary task for the description,
analysis, and resolution of the conflict between life and death. The
new paradigm requires that the church consider its role in the
various conflicts and opt for life, especially supporting the poor in
their struggle for life. Previously the church's role was seen as
primarily serving as a cushion in the midst of conflicts or as a
supporter of the status quo. This chapter explores the nature and
challenge of liberation theologies in the context of Latin America
and the current reappraisal of their impact in North America. My
evaluation is from the perspective of the North American Hispanic
community, whose voice is just beginning to be heard in the wider
global Christian community. A brief description of the historical
background of Latin America will help to set the context for exploring liberation theologies.

Historical Background

The history of Latin American nations represents a varied tapestry, but certain commonalities can be identified. Social, economic, and political issues loom as important in this history because of the cross-currents of foreign influence that have swept across the Americas. The people of Latin America have been identified as a "cosmic race," with the distinctive blending of Amerindian, African, and European (primarily Spanish and Portuguese) cultures. In discussing Latin American history, one must first acknowledge the significance of Amerindian nations who originally migrated south from Asia through the Americas. Enrique Dussel, a major historian of Latin America, has identified three major periods in post-Columbian Latin American history:[1] the colonial period (1492–1808), the decline of Christendom and rise of pluralism (1808–1962), and the break with Christendom and the rise of a new spirit of liberation (1962–present). The economic, political, and cultural conquests of the colonial period were closely tied with the imposition of Christianity. The patronage system of Spanish landlords was legitimated by the transplantation of Spanish religious forms and practices with little recognition of indigenous culture. The decline of Christendom paralleled the rise of primarily secular independence and national movements, as was described for Ecuador in the introduction. Along with these movements came "neo-colonialism," an increasing dependence upon the North Atlantic community. In the period following 1962, Latin Americans have seriously questioned the terms of neo-colonialism and rejected the developmentalism that resulted in a decreased quality of life for the vast majority of common folk as they confronted a host of destroyers in the land.

Destroyers in the Land

The questions explicitly and implicitly asked by Latin Americans in formulating a new theological paradigm are: "Who are the giants in the land?" and "Who are the destroyers of life?" In response to such questions, a host of destroyers can be named that have plagued people and communities for many years. But of these destroyers, Guillermo Cook has identified eight with particular impact in Latin America.[2] While identifying and describing these eight destroyers in order to depict the socioeconomic conditions in much of Latin America, we must also recognize that, in fact, their names are legion and that they represent a major challenge for the church of Jesus Christ at the close of the twentieth century—not only in Latin America but globally.

Among the destroyers of life are ever-present poverty and marginalization, which for many have been connected with economic dependence upon the United States and Western Europe, the North Atlantic community, and Japan. This connection is made because of exorbitant external debt and corresponding high inflation, which result in very limited resources being allocated for local needs in order to repay the staggering foreign debt. Evidences of this poverty were apparent on my travels in Ecuador and Nicaragua. My daughter will never forget walking one evening in Cuenca, Ecuador, and finding a young indigenous boy sleeping alone on the street.

In relation to this first destroyer, the stance of liberation theologians is often described as opting for the poor—an identification with and advocacy for the needs of the vast numbers of poor folk in Latin America, whose lot has worsened over the past several years. The discoveries of Gustavo Gutierrez in working with the poor are helpful in understanding this first destroyer. José Miguez Bonino thus summarized Gutierrez's account of his discoveries:

> I discovered three things. I discovered that poverty was a destructive thing, something to be fought against and destroyed, not merely something which was the object of our charity. Secondly, I discovered that poverty was not accidental. The fact that these people are poor and not rich is not just a matter of chance, but the result of a structure. It was a structural question. Thirdly, I discovered that poor people were a social class. When I discovered that poverty was something to be fought against, that poverty was structural, that poor people were a

class, it became crystal clear that in order to serve the
poor, one had to move into political action.[3]

In response to such poverty, the words of Dom Helder Camara
are sobering: "When I give food to the poor, they call me a saint.
When I ask why the poor have no food, they call me a communist."
A second destroyer is the devastation of ethnic cultures, the
devaluing of indigenous people and their way of life. This cultural
destruction deprives people of a sense of their past and a crucial
foundation for their identity. One purpose of my journey was to
recover aspects of my cultural past in Ecuador, and yet ironically
this opportunity is not afforded many now living in Latin America.
This cultural imperialism is not unlike the primal crime of U.S.
history that devastated a host of Amerindian peoples and their
cultures. One example of this devaluation of ethnic cultures was
the disdain expressed by the child of one of my Ecuadorian rela-
tives for the crafts and art works of indigenous people from his own
country.
A third destroyer is the institutional violence and militarization
that exists in much of Latin America. Under the guise of maintaining national security, many regimes have committed human rights
violations, with a high incidence of torture and the disappearance
of persons. Such disappearances create a continuous cycle of suffering for the families and friends of those who have been victimized. I can recall vividly the anguish expressed by an Argen-
tinean woman whose husband and other family members had
disappeared. In a conference on pastoral ministries with families,
held at the Latin American Biblical Seminary in Costa Rica, she
spoke out passionately for the use of a community image for pastoral work since the very naming of "family" brought various associations of pain and loss for many like herself in her country. I also
recall the stories told by Central American women who were repeatedly raped throughout their journeys from their countries of
origin through Mexico to the border of the United States. These
crimes were often committed by government representatives who
intercepted refugees during their travels, robbing them of their
money and their dignity.

Thus, based upon such accounts, the fourth destroyer can be identified as devaluation of human life itself, rampant in various ways. Persons with limited resources—very often women and children—are viewed as expendable. Visiting both a land-invasion community and a *maquiladora* (a factory at the U.S./Mexico border) in July 1990, I was reminded of the many communities I had encountered and studied on my earlier travels in Latin America. Decisions were and are being made that daily lessen the possibilities of many people to have viable lives free from hunger, disease, ignorance, and personal alienation.

A fifth destroyer of the fabric of common life is the ideological manipulation of the truth by means of mass communication. Having visited the May Day celebration in the Plaza of the Revolution in downtown Managua, Nicaragua, in 1989, I was amazed to read three accounts of this very same event. One description in the government paper, then controlled by the Sandinistas, grossly exaggerated the size of the crowd present and the generally positive mood of the occasion. By contrast, the opposition paper discounted the event as a small gathering, vastly underestimating the numbers present and characterizing the speeches in a very negative fashion that ignored the speakers' call for national reconciliation. The third account, which I read in a Costa Rican paper upon my return there, stressed a violent rejection of anything associated with the Sandinistas' Nicaragua and reported a negative reaction to peace efforts that was not voiced in the public event I witnessed. Although I recognized the influence of the reporters' personal and political biases, I was hard-pressed to imagine that these three accounts were of the same event that I witnessed.

A sixth destroyer is the systematic destruction of the environment, not only for current generations, but for many generations to come. In the introduction, I discussed the problem of deforestation in Costa Rica. In Managua, I was most impressed by Lake Managua, which sits at the base of the city and could become a center for the recreational needs of the ever-expanding population in this urban center. This possibility was discounted by the extremely high pollution levels of the lake, which has become a repository for all of the city's human and industrial waste. The cost of cleanup is

estimated to be in the multimillion dollar range, with little possibility of securing funds given the other pressing national needs.
Such destruction could have been avoided by public attention to the
practices of indigenous peoples, whose use of the land recognizes
its value as a heritage to be made available to succeeding generations.

A seventh destroyer of life as God intended it is the rise of
substance abuse in Latin America. Drug trafficking and use have
become attractive alternatives for many who struggle daily with the
realities of survival. During our visit to Ecuador, we learned that
heightened law-enforcement efforts in Colombia had increased the
presence in Ecuador of Colombian drug interests and the purchase
of Ecuadorian land and chemical companies by Colombian drug
lords. In Ecuador, the legal and enforcement apparatus had not yet
developed sufficiently to address the major threat posed by drug
trafficking. In addition, a number of state policies in Latin America
have supported alcoholism as a means by which to pacify the
population. The personal, familial, and economic havoc perpetuated by such substance abuse has been cited by various observers.
The physical and psychological abuse suffered by women and children due to alcoholism in their families has been of epidemic
proportion.

The rise of prostitution in urban centers and a corresponding
dissolution of family life represents an eighth destroyer. Prostitution has become an economic necessity for a number of women
who have not had available alternative means of economic support.
With the departure or disappearance of the working male in house-
holds, the issue of survival becomes primary. With a steady stream
of humanity from rural and agricultural settings to urban centers,
the extended-family network has often been broken, with a great
loss of needed support. The additional tragedy in this situation is
the loss of what is most highly valued in Latin culture, namely the
family itself. The value of the family will be discussed in further
detail in chapter 5.

Other destroyers may be named, including governmental corrup-
tion and a general sense of alienation across all levels of society.
Not listed among these eight destroyers of life is the church itself,

which has often explicitly and implicitly participated in the culture of death. The complicity of the Christian church represents a scandal calling for repentance and conversion on the part of Christians in both North and Latin America. But the church's recognition of these eight destroyers and their impact serves to indicate that the physical, social, and spiritual struggle for life against the forces of death is a daily reality. For the vast majority of people, survival is an ever-present concern. Therefore, in Latin America, the primary dilemma confronting Christians is the significance of the gospel as an alternative to a culture of death and destruction rampant in society. The life, death, and resurrection of Jesus Christ are seen in relation to the life, death, and potential resurrection of people and communities who daily confront the destroyers of life. Christians are called to clarify their commitments in relation to these destroyers and to consider the call for liberation that has been sounded in Latin America.

The Church's Response: A Call for Liberation

In relation to these destroyers or demonic forces at work in Latin American society, the question is asked, "What is God's will?" Three distinct perspectives in response to this question have been named by Irene Foulkes, who was serving as the dean of the Latin American Biblical Seminary when she welcomed my family and me at the airport in Costa Rica. These three perspectives have characterized the church's reaction to the world. The first has been described as a world-denying perspective, which refuses to analyze societal realities that represent a world system in rebellion against God and slated for destruction in God's reign. This perspective dictates that the appropriate Christian response is therefore to deny the world and to remain apart from it to maintain a secure community that is not "of" the world. The second perspective has been described as a world-affirming one. This perspective seeks to identify with the world, to name its realities, and to celebrate one's position in it. The appropriate Christian response from this second perspective is, therefore, to embrace the world with its contradictions and to accept full participation and citizenship in a world created by God and through which God has chosen our pilgrimage. The third perspective has been named as one that seeks to transform the world. This perspective seeks to correct those realities and to right the wrongs that make participation in the world as it now exists problematic.[4]

The appropriate Christian response implied by Foulkes's description is to diligently and cooperatively work for the transformation of those realities in need of change while maintaining a stance of being *in* but not *of* the world. Given the realities described above, the option increasingly voiced in Latin America is one that seeks to transform the world by the grace of God and the power of the Holy Spirit to a closer conformity of God's will as revealed in the reign of Jesus Christ. God's will is discerned as seeking the full liberation of people, communities, and societies. But opting for transformation and liberation poses the questions of how to bring about change and in what forms change may take place so that liberation, and not alternative forms of oppression, may be experienced.

Levels of Liberation

The task of liberation can be seen in relation to three distinct levels identified by Gustavo Gutierrez which, though distinct, are intimately connected. The first level of liberation is socioeconomic and political, seeking the empowerment and release of the oppressed, the exploited classes, despised ethnic groups, and marginalized cultures, who must receive full access to resources they need to live. This level represents the aspiration of all oppressed people. In relation to this level, the church is called to a ministry of advocacy for and identification with those who are voiceless and powerless under current societal arrangements. The second level of liberation is anthropological, calling for a qualitatively different society. This second level represents a distinct understanding of history, in which persons assume conscious responsibility for their destinies. Cooperation, partnership, and the worth of each person's life are the values affirmed at this level. Each individual is viewed as having dignity and worth, deserving care and concern, throughout life and even in death. In relation to this level, the church is called upon to model a community of care and concern for all persons. The third level of liberation is theological and spiritual, calling for the liberation from sin, which is viewed as the ultimate root of all injustice and oppression. This third level includes communion with God. All three levels of liberation are seen by Gutierrez as part of God's one salvific process.[5] This theological and spiritual liberation enables people to fully embrace a life of community and participation in fulfilling God's mission in the world.

Various theologians of liberation elaborate upon these levels and relate their characteristics from their own unique perspectives. But what transcends their various efforts is the attempt to grapple with the stark realities of Latin America in a faithful response to the radical demands of the gospel of Jesus Christ. Some would relegate the church's role to just the theological and spiritual level, but many liberation theologians call for a holistic response that incorporates actions at all three levels. One person who has spoken about such a holistic response is Guillermo Cook, who at the time of my visit to Costa Rica, was working with the Latin American Evangelical Center for Pastoral Studies (CELEP), co-founded by Orlando Costas.

Guillermo Cook has insightfully addressed the question, "What is the mission of the church in Latin America?" In addressing this question, Cook suggests that the church should respond to the realities in Latin America by becoming a prophetic, priestly, and political people, paralleling the threefold mission of Jesus Christ in the world as prophet, priest, and king. But Cook has reinterpreted the usual associations with the threefold office of Christ in relation to Latin American realities. A prophetic people is called to incarnate gospel values in the community and society. A priestly people is called to a life of sacrificial giving and a pastoral vocation that includes both clergy and laity. A political people is called to a life of service for the public.[6] It is in relation to this mission that Cook and Orlando Costas, both missiologists, have sought to develop a theology of liberation.

Orlando Costas liked to describe *mission* as the mother of theology, as might be expected from the perspective of his work as a missiologist.[7] A perspective I would affirm as a practical theologian is that *mission* and *theology* become partners along with *education* in fostering the response of the whole people of God to the call of Christ in Latin America and in the world. The question of mothering and fathering, of queening and kinging (if one thinks of theology as the queen of the sciences, with philosophy as her handmaiden) must be seen in relation to the pressing needs to minister faithfully in a global context of great need and rapid change. Such a stance does not negate the crucial question of one's authority in ministry, mission, and theology, but seeks to foster a cooperative and collaborative effort across the theological disciplines, which on occasion have been estranged. From the perspective of a practical theologian, this may be accomplished readily with the emphasis upon Christian religious education being seen as an art and craft more than as a science.

In theological dialogue, one becomes aware of varying perspectives that may limit the possibility of learning from others. Historically this has been the case between North and South America, but the reality of globalization calls for careful consideration of what can be learned from the informed engagement of Latin American Christians in relation to liberation movements. One insight that emerges from dialogue between the North and South, with their divergent perspectives, is the place of ideology and theology in the theory and practice of Christian education. Such an insight requires critical assessment of the theology and ideology implicit in Christian education itself.

Perspectives from the North and South

In understanding the differences between North and South America in relation to theology and world view, the work of Leonardo Boff in *Jesus Christ the Liberator* is insightful. Boff describes five paired theological polarities with Latin Americans giving primacy to the first term in each pair. First, in Latin America, *anthropology* is stressed over *ecclesiology.* In other words, the focus of attention is not on the church itself but on human beings and their life in society. The church is called to raise up and humanize people and to advocate for the needs of all humanity given the ever-present devaluation of human life. Second, Latin Americans emphasize the *utopian* view over the *factual* view. Although at first glance this perspective may appear to be in conflict with the naming of realities described as a necessary first step, here the subsequent and long-term view is of concern and the future is of greater interest than the present. The reign of God in history is anticipated, and the emergence of a new humanity, which itself is in the process of coming to birth, is a priority. Third, a *critical* or problem-posing stance is stressed over a *dogmatic* or problem-solving stance. This has been the case because the core of liberation and the radical transformation it requires have not been adequately discerned and grasped. As a result of this lack of discernment and commitment, a dogmatic or problem-solving approach to the realities has maintained and legitimated the status quo in Latin America. Fourth, the *social* and *public* dimension of life has been stressed over the *personal* dimension. Thus, the secular and public implications of the gospel message of Jesus have received greater attention among those who espouse some form of liberation theology. One insightful warning that was issued by Father Miguel Ramos in Ecuador regarding this emphasis on social concerns was that the need for personal transformation must not be forgotten. He observed that changes in the structures of society is not complete unless transformation also occurs in the people who form those structures and perpetuate them. Fifth, in Latin America, *orthopraxis,* right action or practice, has been emphasized over *orthodoxy,* right thought.[8] Truth is viewed as a verb in this emphasis on the praxiological element in the message of Christ. José Miguez Bonino has emphasized this perspective in asserting that the goal of truth is not just intelligence but faithful obedience to the will of God.[9]

In contrast with the emphasis on the first term in each of the five pairs named above from a Latin American liberation perspective, church culture in the United States has generally opted for the second term. Thus, in the United States, emphasis has been placed on ecclesiology over anthropology, the factual over the utopian, the dogmatic over the critical, the personal over the social, and orthodoxy over orthopraxis. With such contrasting but potentially complementary theological emphases between the North and South in the Americas, the need for dialogue and interaction is evident from the vantage point of a North American Hispanic practical theologian. Too often, the choice of alternative theological values has led to polarization and division rather than an opportunity for dialogue and an agreement to disagree, especially on complementary elements of the faith. This choice has also prevented people from seeing the multifaceted dimensions of God's truth.

The challenge of the gospel impacts upon each of the terms in the five pairs named above and any other that might be suggested. One insight I gained from my travels in Latin America is that Christians have much more to share in common than they have to divide and fragment them. In addition, I relearned that God's truth is multifaceted and that no one Christian group has a monopoly on that truth. Thus, there is a continuing need among Christians for ecumenical dialogue and for a willingness to admit that they may be mistaken regarding a theological principle. This willingness implicitly recognizes that "ever new light and truth break forth from God's holy Word" in our time.[10] A refusal to dialogue limits the work of the Holy Spirit to reveal new understandings and to correct past and current excesses in theological matters. Such a refusal also denies the work of the church in confessing the mystery of the faith, which is spoken of as "the pillar and bulwark of the truth" in 1 Tim. 3:15–16.[11] For the church in its global reality to be confessing anything it must be in dialogue across national, cultural, political, gender, and theological borders. For the truth to be discerned and disclosed by the church, conversation is needed between the North and South in the Americas and beyond.

Questions of Suffering and Solidarity

During my eight-month journey in Latin America, I became acutely aware of the extent of suffering experienced by the common folk. This suffering is a result of their daily encounter with the destroyers of life that have been identified above. Suffering itself and the naming of its presence is also a distinctive of Latin consciousness. But the naming of suffering experienced in various forms does call forth a human and theological response, referred to in Latin America is as *"solidaridad"* or solidarity. Solidarity refers to the willingness to stand with those who are suffering, to identify with their plight, and to be willing to advocate their causes toward the alleviation of suffering. It also refers to taking sides with the poor and oppressed or to making a choice to support them in one's life and ministry.

A stance of solidarity assumes that the poor and oppressed have not had the power and voice to advocate their perspective and to work for constructive change. Thus if one stands in solidarity with the poor, one is also called to work for the empowerment of those who have been marginalized and excluded from society and often from the church itself. In naming empowerment, one must recognize that only God ultimately empowers persons. A stance of solidarity requires a shift in focus from ministry *to* and *for* the poor to a ministry *with* and *of* the poor. This shift requires a concerted effort to equip the poor themselves so that they may speak and work in the world to transform those realities that perpetuate their poverty. Differences arise as to how this might be done. But such a shift implies the need for perceptual and structural conversion on the part of people communities, and societal systems. Anything less results in the maintenance of the status quo and an unwillingness to embrace the full liberation required to make a difference in the life of the poor.

Solidarity fosters a reassurance that God sees, hears, and will respond because others see, hear, and respond. God works through human beings and is seen through their efforts. Solidarity fosters a reassurance that God is indeed present through the ministry of the Holy Spirit, who accompanies and empowers people in the midst of their suffering. Because God is present, solidarity implies a willingness to take risks, to be supportive, and to share the agony experienced by others. The apostle Paul described this experience of solidarity in 2 Cor. 4:7–12:

> But we have this treasure in clay jars, so that it may be made clear that this extraordinary power belongs to God and does not come from us. We are afflicted in every

way, but not crushed; perplexed, but not driven to despair; persecuted, but not forsaken; struck down, but not destroyed; always carrying in the body the death of Jesus, so that the life of Jesus may also be made visible in our bodies. For while we live, we are always being given up to death for Jesus' sake, so that the life of Jesus may be made visible in our mortal flesh. So death is at work in us, but life in you.

A stance of solidarity with others in their suffering involves a willingness to bear the death of Jesus and the commonality of his suffering (Phil. 3:10) in our own lives with the assurance of God's comfort and consolation (2 Cor. 1:3-7). The apostle Peter is reported to have named this experience as sharing in the very suffering of Christ, which can result in rejoicing (1 Pet. 4:13). The reality of this experience of solidarity is captured by the popular saying that "a joy shared is twice the joy, and a sorrow shared is half the sorrow."

A commitment to human solidarity embodies a willingness to be touched by the human suffering, affliction, and oppression of others. When comforts in the United States lead to the discomfort of current and future generations in the world, serious questions must be raised. A faith in Jesus Christ demands that Christians in North America hear the cries for justice emerging from Latin America. Abraham Heschel, a Jewish educator, in his work *The Prophets*, provided insights to assist in appreciating the prophetic voices from Central and South America. Heschel observed that justice dies when it is deified, for beyond justice is God's compassion. He maintained that justice is a mode of action that addresses the outside of our life and that righteousness is the quality of a person that addresses the inside of our life.[12] Our response to God in terms of the inside and outside of our lives comes to represent the call for integrity in our faith and life. Heschel further observed that righteousness goes beyond justice because justice is strict and exact, whereas righteousness implies benevolence, kindness, and generosity. Nevertheless, the concern for justice is an act of love or compassion and an expression of righteousness.[13] From a Christian perspective, the righteousness described is not one of our own making, which Isaiah graphically describes as filthy rags (Isa. 64:6), but a righteousness gifted to us in Jesus Christ. With this gracious gift, North Americans are called to stand in solidarity with their sisters and brothers of the western hemisphere who cry for justice to our one God.

The Land

Human solidarity also embraces a theology in which the land is viewed as a heritage for the entire community. By virtue of the creation and human stewardship of God's world, indigenous peoples and communities in Latin America remind us that the land is our mother and must be treated with respect and love. Thus solidarity includes a solidarity with the creation, which is also in bondage and seeking liberation from abuse and exploitation. A call is issued to care for and protect the land. Just as we would not, under normal circumstances, abuse our parents, we must not abuse the land, which is the common heritage of our own generation and generations to come. Thus the human community and all of creation comprise an interlocking network of interdependent relationships that must be recognized and honored.

A commitment to solidarity that embraces the land embodies a commitment to future generations. Once a society invests more in its self-gratification and survival than in the education and well-being of future generations, it is liable to social bankruptcy. Signs of this bankruptcy are evident in the United States. Countries like Costa Rica and Ecuador are highly committed to the education of all their citizens. We in the United States have lacked this commitment for a number of years, with devastating results in terms of increased resources being required for penal systems and social services. Many religious communities are inadequately supporting the education of clerical and lay leaders and persons across the life span; similarly, they are inadequately investing in their future scholars and professors. More support is needed to insure the perpetuation of dynamic church and social life.

El Cuco

Why is the issue of human solidarity so crucial in Latin America? Given the existence of clear social-class demarcations and the separation of people from differing social classes, the recognition that all people are human and worthy of respect, love, and care can be revolutionary. I recall a mural my cousin painted in the house on the family *quinta* or farm outside of Quito, Ecuador, where the family held a gathering. The *quinta* is cared for by a poor indigenous family. The children of my extended family are fearful of the mural and call it *el cuco,* which can be translated the "monster" or "bogeyman." It depicts a high wall with a locked metal gate, viewed from the inside. Outside the gate is amassed a large company of indigenous people, pressed closely together and waiting to enter. In this mass of humanity, the faces of only those in the front row, crushed against the gate, can be seen with their penetrating and desperate expressions. All the others are depicted as a faceless but ever-present body of humanity for which one must account. The cousin who painted the mural did not return to Ecuador for many years.

The image of that gate will remain with me in relation to a challenge named by Orlando Costas. In his work *Christ Outside the Gate,* Costas refers to the scriptural passage Heb. 13:7–16, in which Jesus is described as one who suffered outside the city gate in order to sanctify the people by his own blood and who in turn invites Christians to join him outside and bear the abuse he endured.[14] The depiction of the scene outside the gate in the mural that so frightened the children mirrored the suffering of Jesus in bearing the costs of a sacrificial ministry. In fact, it is in Christ that the divisions of social class that keep people inside and outside of gates and other barriers have been and are being shattered. Through the ministry of Jesus Christ today, relationships can be established, dialogue can be explored, and a sense of community can be expanded across class lines and the multiple distinctions that divide the human community. Christ's ministry also challenges the privileged classes to assume their responsibility for their sisters and brothers outside the gate so that, unlike Cain, we may be our sisters' and brothers' keepers.

In the United States, we are often blind to social class differences, yet they exist. For example, in 1979 my son applied for admission to Trinity School in New York City, a quality private day school. Before examining our son's qualifications, the admissions officer directed my wife and me to other private schools with higher percentages of minority students. Needless to say, the admissions officer was not aware of our knowledge of these schools or the implications of such a recommendation. Richard de Lone, in his study for the Carnegie Council on Children entitled *Small Futures,* identified a functional caste system in the United States that has isolated lower-class African Americans, American Indians, Mexican Americans, and Puerto Ricans from the mainstream of U.S. life. My wife is Puerto Rican, and I feel Puerto Rican by virtue of being adopted into her family. Today we speak of the "permanent underclass" and do not shudder at what that implies for the steadily increasing numbers of children born to such families in an era of reduced government spending for social programs. Therefore, the issue of human solidarity must be raised even in the United States, where growing gaps exist in the availability of basic human services such as food, clothing, housing, health care, and education. Such gaps directly impact upon the quality of life for children who must be viewed as the children of all of us.

The realities of suffering, deprivation, and oppression are daily occurrences, and the gospel calls for a response to such realities with the love of Christ and meeting the needs of the whole person—body, soul, and spirit. The diaconal ministry of the Christian church embodies a response that offers the choice of life and the promotion of life for all God's creatures, especially for those discarded by society as a permanent underclass. Those so identified are precious in the sight of God and are worthy of love, respect, care, and service in the name of Christ. Gospel values are in direct conflict with the values embodied in the world, which emphasize political, social, and economic power as the principal attributes of human worth.

A Challenge for All

The New Testament book of Philemon provides a challenge for rich and poor alike, as was explained by an Ecuadorian seminarian who spoke at the Emaús community in Costa Rica one Sunday morning. Philemon, the rich slave owner had to recognize a common humanity, a solidarity, with his runaway slave, Onesimus, who is named as Paul the apostle's son in the faith. Since Philemon was a partner with Paul, one can imagine the offense for Philemon to refuse to accept his partner's son as an equal and to care for him as such. A challenge is also presented to Onesimus, however, who is called to recognize his dignity and responsibility in relation to Philemon and ultimately in relation to God. The challenges or conversions called for by both Philemon and Onesimus are significant in the appropriation of their full humanity and the solidarity with others of a different estate. A similar challenge is posed for the rich and poor of the Americas.

The response of liberation theologies in Latin America has been to take seriously the human condition that calls for a Christian reappropriation of the incarnation. Liberation theologies can be seen in part as a new effort to formulate a Christian humanism in tune with new sociological, political, and economic understandings of the human dilemma as experienced by many segments of the global community outside of North America and Western Europe. A Christian response in the face of the destroyers of life named above is to keep life uniquely human as intended by God, particularly in the face of extensive poverty, oppression, injustice, and war. The distinctive character of Christian humanization affirms that every person is made in the image of God, has intrinsic and eternal worth, and can realize his or her full potential in following Jesus the Savior. Given this reality, every person is to be respected, cared for, and not abused or exploited. This humanization has been too readily overlooked in the United States, but times of economic hardship may bring about a greater recognition of the needs of others to counter the prevalent egoistic individualism. A reappropriation of the incarnation in the face of poverty involves a willingness to recognize and identify with those who suffer in the same way that Jesus left the riches of his inheritance to become poor for our sake (2 Corinthians 8:9). The formulations of liberation theologians, like all theologians who seek to study God and express their love of God, are subject to excesses and limitations.

However, their intentions and motivations include a commitment to incarnate the Christian gospel amid the struggles of people and communities in the Americas. Struggles include those for daily survival and the provision of life against death in its manifest forms. These struggles are named from the perspective of those who are marginalized and who occupy the base of the socio-economic scale, having little or no voice or power in the determinative affairs of modern society. They are the least of our sisters and brothers in the human community, those of whom Jesus spoke in describing the judgment of the nations (Matt. 25:40): "Truly I tell you, just as you did it to one of the least of these who are members of my family, you did it to me."

The denial of, disdain for, or indifference to the suffering of others by North American society in general is a sin. The failure to be touched by the infirmities of others brings God's judgment. But the sensitivity to, identification with, and empathy with the suffering experienced by Latin Americans does not itself bring salvation; rather, it can occasion an openness to the salvation offered by God. What then are sin and salvation in the light of the challenges posed by liberation theologians?

Sin goes deeper than class distinctions and the division between the rich and the poor, though conflicts between social and economic classes are expressions of social sin. For some liberation theologians, sin is equated with capitalism as an economic system and the resulting death and alienation caused by this system in Latin America. But for others, sin is a more radical condition that involves alienation from God, ourselves, others, and the entire created order. Salvation embodies the restoration and transformation of our relationship with God, others, ourselves, and the created order. Suffering can lead to bitterness; hopelessness; resignation; despair; and violence directed against oneself, one's family, and others. Suffering in and of itself and its naming do not bring salvation. Repudiation of the North American system and its idols of comfort, success, and pleasure associated with the accumulation of material possessions does not bring salvation. As much as this condemnation and prophetic utterance must be heard in relation to North American idols, the transformation and conversion described in the gospel as salvation embraces all of life and the questioning of any system with alternative values, whether it be capitalistic or socialistic. The excesses of liberation theologies have included close identification with Marxist ideology and socialist arrangements to the exclusion of constructive criticism and the work for justice and righteousness within socialist systems themselves.

A Conflict of Values: North and South

A conflict of values can be identified in comparing realities in the United States and Latin America and the response to suffering. In North America, the danger exists of sacrificing the prophetic dimension of the Christian faith for the pragmatic and the reasonable. In Latin America, the danger exists of sacrificing the reasonable and the pragmatic for the prophetic. Gabriel García Marquez described the differences in a distinctive and insightful way. He observed that in North America we contend with the poverty of abundance, but in Latin America we contend with the abundance of poverty. Although we view global realities from different angles and address suffering from different contexts, we nevertheless share the challenge of living together with peace and justice in one world. This challenge was posed for me in a relationship with a Costa Rican friend named Trinidad.

Trinidad, or "Trini" as she was affectionately known to her friends, was a fifty-year-old woman we met the first day we arrived in Costa Rica. Trini had come to welcome us to the community and to graciously offer her services to us as a domestic worker. We had never had a servant in our home, and so we thanked Trini for her offer but initially explained to her that we could not afford her services. Two months later, we received additional funds and were able to have Trini work four hours a week, assisting us with cooking and light housework. My own responsibilities included the heavy housework. By this time, Trini had become so close a friend that my wife often cleaned the house prior to Trini's weekly visit so as to have time to talk with her while they cooked together. Trini was a charismatic Roman Catholic laywoman who for two months in late 1988 had pursued her girlhood dream by entering a convent as a novice. Convent life did not suit Trini's style of lay ministry, and she returned—embarrassed but with conscious relief—to her previous life. One day, Trini came to our home with a large bruise on her arm. Her injury had occurred while working in another home. She said that she thanked God for her pain and celebrated her suffering as a reminder of all that Jesus had suffered for us. Although from a North American perspective, Trini's insight might be seen as masochistic, for her it was a significant spiritual experience of God's grace in the midst of her physical suffering. I expressed my concern for Trini's health and inquired whether her working conditions had caused her fall, but Trini's attention was focused on what her mishap had taught her about Jesus. I was left pondering her response.

Other incidents will serve to highlight the distinct perspectives on suffering I encountered in Latin America. One of our neighbors in *Desamparados* delighted in regaling me, after my car accident, with the details of various auto accidents and their resulting injuries. This recounting, though morbid to my sensitivities at first, signaled a solidarity with others who had suffered and a thankfulness to God that my accident was not worse. Portrayals of the bleeding and wounded hearts of Jesus and Mary were ever present in the popular and visual arts in Costa Rica and Ecuador. These portrayals support the idea that God is present with us in the midst of our suffering. Finally, I recall seeing persons of various ages walking long distances on their knees to the Cathedral of Cartago, where the icon of the patron saint of Costa Rica is housed. This portrayed for the participants the seriousness of commitment and petition for the various needs of common folk. The naming and embracing of suffering, along with God's identification with this suffering, are very characteristic of Latin personal and religious culture. Thus it has become a theme in the response of liberation theologians who live and work in Latin America. The reality of the cross is taken seriously in an appreciation of Jesus' suffering and God's identification with human suffering.

Three Phases of Suffering

Dorothee Soelle, in her work entitled *Suffering*, has identified three phases of suffering, and it is helpful to distinguish responses to these phases in North and South America. The first phase is that of silence, in which a passive acceptance of the victims' suffering is maintained. In the United States, this phase has been exemplified by many, including the poor, children, and (until recently) women. The silence phase can also be seen in a failure of North Americans to recognize that our prosperity is too often maintained at the expense of many in Latin America. The second phase is the awareness and articulation of the suffering, in which victims speak out and refuse to be victimized. Such breaking of the silence and lamenting the oppression has occurred in Latin America in the voices of liberation theologians but can unfortunately remain fixated at this phase. The third phase is the active organization to transform the conditions causing the suffering and to envision new possibilities for people, communities, and societies.[15] This third phase is a challenge to be addressed jointly by those in both the North and South of the Americas. In Latin America, the response to suffering has led some to consider the insights of Marxism.

The Appeal of Marxism and Reactions

As Latin Americans have addressed the challenge of alleviating suffering and transforming the conditions that have caused the suffering, some have turned to Marxism to gain insights. The appropriation of Marxism has been problematic with the recent demise of communism in Eastern Europe and the Soviet Union, but exploring its impact upon some theologies of liberation is helpful. In considering the relationship between Marxism and liberation theologies, it is important to bear in mind the following three distinctions, made by Robert McAfee Brown in *Theology in a New Key*. First, Marxism often appears as a religio-philosophical movement based on atheistic ideology. Few if any liberation theologians appeal to Marxism in this sense. A strict Marxist conception of life is reductionistic. Similar to a strict capitalist and market-based analysis, Marxism sees life mainly in terms of economic forces, which are determinative for all of life. Second, Marxism offers a political strategy designed to overcome glaring class inequities and discrepancies. In general, liberation theologians advocate revolutionary action only in view of unyielding systemic injustice and only after exhausting whatever peaceful means are available to disen-franchised people. Third, Marxism brings with it a set of tools for societal analysis based on the principle of class conflict.[16] Recog-nizing the various levels of conflict that have been described in relation to the destroyers of life rampant in Latin America, one can readily understand an interest in Marxist conflict analysis. Those involved in the liberation movement have concluded that such methodologies offer the hope of making sense out of Latin Ameri-can realities and for proposing alternatives for exploited peoples condemned to looking at the world from the bottom up. For some under socialist political systems, this alternative has led to a new bondage in which human freedoms are denied. The value of these freedoms must be understood in relation to the need for survival. It is primarily in this third sense that Marxism plays a significant role in many liberation theologies while recognizing the distinctive at-tributes of the Christian faith.

While proclaiming the emergence of liberation theologies in Latin America, one must recognize that not all Christian people or communities affirm this theological stance. In Costa Rica, I en-countered a large number of conservative or evangelical Christians who viewed the espousal of any liberation theology as a heretical distortion of the gospel. While in Central America, I received a document published by a group of conservative Protestant church leaders who met in August 1988 to discuss their reactions to the challenges of liberation theology in what was called the "Medellin Consultation 88." Some conference organizers had hoped that this consultation would result in a resounding denunciation of liberation theology in Latin America, reversing the affirmation the movement had received in 1968 at the Second General Conference of Latin American Bishops. The 1988 document, entitled the "The Medellin Declaration of Liberation Theology," made observations regarding the theology of liberation and confessed the lack of response on the part of many conservative Christian communities to the various needs of the people in Latin America.[17] It named the excesses of some liberation theologies but did not denounce the genuine effort to respond faithfully to the host of destroyers of life with the message of the gospel of Jesus Christ. The document sounded a note of reconciliation not often heard between contending theological camps in Latin America and signaled hope for future dialogue.

This hope is also sounded in the work of Samuel Solivan, a North American Hispanic systematic theologian who has had missionary experience in Latin America. Solivan maintains that a new paradigm is needed in the dialogue between the Americas and between conservative and liberation theologies. Conservative theology stresses the need for orthodoxy, right belief or creed, and the continuity of Christian faith with the gospel as preserved through the ages. In contrast, liberation theology stresses the need for praxis or orthopraxis, right practice and reflection on that practice of faith, and the discontinuity of faithful responses to the challenges of contemporary life in contrast with perpetuating the status quo. These differences can result in an irreconcilable conflict in relation to the priorities of faith that may not recognize the need for *both* orthodoxy *and* orthopraxis. Solivan suggests that a third conversation partner, "orthopathos," must be introduced. Orthopathos is the right response of feeling, passion, and commitment to address the realities of suffering and to destroy the destroyers of life, a response that calls forth the best of Christian thinking and belief and the best of Christian practice and action.[18] Anything less reduces the gospel and fails to give glory to God.

An encounter with advocates of liberation theologies in Latin America during my journey enabled me to consider new challenges for the Christian church in North America and, in particular, what might be suggested for the transformation of Christian education in both its theory and practice. New questions must be raised in relation to old alliances and formulas. This transformation seeks to combine the insights from both orthodoxy and orthopraxis with an orthopathos that addresses the genuine needs of people in all the Americas. The transformation of Christian education as theorists and practitioners respond to new global challenges is the subject of chapters 2 and 3, which seek to wrestle with and build upon the insights gained from the encounter with liberation theologies. Although recent North American discussions of liberation theology have frequently dismissed its relevance to the Christian church, I think this is a grave mistake. However, it does suggest the need for reappraisal.

A Reappraisal

With the fall of communism as practiced in Eastern Europe and the Soviet Union, much publicity has been given to the demise of Marxism and liberation theologies that have drawn upon Marxist analysis for some of their insights. Serious questions can also be posed in relation to the demise of capitalism during times of recession and depression in the world economy. The moral and spiritual legacy of capitalism must likewise be questioned as former communist nations rush toward capitalism. The wholesale dismissal of liberation theologies is premature because it fails to address the continued presence of the destroyers of life throughout Latin America and the world. The limitations and excesses of some expressions of liberation theology certainly must be acknowledged in their failure to recognize the demonic possibilities of socialist as well as capitalist systems along with the severe limitations of Marxist analysis. Father Miguel Ramos's insight must also be mentioned again, namely that transformation must impact upon the personal lives of those who occupy positions in renewed societal structures and systems if change is to be sustained and new oppressions avoided. To stress only systemic and structural change is as reductionistic as to stress only personal and communal change.

To totally discount the challenges posed by liberation theologies for the thought and life of the Christian church in North America is to deny our wider social, political, and ideological commitments as they are shaped by the gospel of Jesus Christ, which calls us to a life of righteousness and justice. This does not entail embracing a socialist, communist, or capitalist agenda, but calls Christians to wrestle with how their faith speaks to the condition of the mass of people who are poor and who seek liberation at all levels of their lives. Our response to those outside the gate, as portrayed in the painting at my family's farmhouse, embodies our response to the

Jesus we encounter in the human needs of the least of our sisters and brothers.

The continuing challenge posed for the church in North America is captured in a parable entitled "Prepare before me a table," written by Guillermo Cook:

> It is as though a large number of people were huddled under a large, food-laden table. They can smell the food, but all they see is the underside, the base of the table. Only a privileged few are seated around that table enjoying the fullness of nature's bounty. Some are totally unconscious of what is happening underneath the table. Others are dimly aware of it and occasionally pass down some crumbs to those below. But several banqueters know well enough who is under the table but are doing their best—and worst—to keep things as they are. They don't want anyone to spoil their meal. Then a person enters the room. He walks across to the table. But instead of taking his place in the seat of honor, he stoops down and gets under the table. He sits with the hopeless people down below and shows them his love and concern. With him as their Head, they begin to have hope. God loves them! God has something good in store for them! They join in small groups to sing, pray, and study His Word. In time they will be ready to come out from under the table to join the privileged few in a common meal around the table.
>
> There is sufficient food to go around. Perhaps not enough for everyone to gorge on, but certainly sufficient to satisfy the basic needs of everyone-if those who are abundantly blessed are only willing to share what they have. But if the banqueters resist, if they should resort to force to keep the others down, it might become necessary, as a last resort, for those under the table to turn it upside down—as Jesus upset the tables of the money-changers in the temple. Of his followers it is written, "These men who have turned the world upside down

have come here also (Acts 17:6)—actually, in the end, to turn things right side up."[19]

As a Christian educator, I will address the challenge of the table in relation to the implications of liberation theology for education, the focus of chapter 2.

The Implications
of Liberation Theology
for Education

The approach of liberation theologies from its Latin roots has direct implications for the theory and practice of religious education in general and of theological education in particular. I propose to consider these implications by using a form of analysis I developed in *Principles and Practices of Christian Education.*[1] In that work, I identified two underlying forms and two complementary principles for Christian education. The first form is the educational trinity of content, persons, and the context of the community/society. In fact, education can be defined as the process of sharing content with people in the context of their community and society. The second form is the five-task model that will be explored in chapter 3 in proposing an educational approach. This second form distinguishes Christian education from education in general. The first principle I identify is that of transformation or conversion, which will also be discussed in chapter 3. It, like the five-task model, distinguishes Christian education in terms of the spiritual interest focused on the person and work of Jesus Christ. The second principle is that of connection. This second principle stresses the need for a holistic educational approach that avoids reductionisms of various sorts. In this chapter, the implications of liberation theologies for education will be evaluated in relation to both the underlying form of the educational trinity and the organizing principle of connection.

As a religious educator, I am committed in theory and practice to a liberating education that is open to the valuable insights of a theology of liberation, while raising a critique of this theological and educational approach. Increasingly, the field of religious education has had to explore its relationships to the theology of liberation within a global context of injustice and oppression.[2] The seminal writings of the Brazilian educator Paulo Freire have confronted religious educators with the need to explore the implications of his work and philosophy for the practice of religious education in the North American church.

Paulo Freire

Paulo Freire was born in 1921 into a middle-class family. Due to financial reverses caused by the American stock-market crash in 1929, he grew up in poverty. He was dedicated to the education and advancement of the poor and oppressed of his native Brazil and to the transformation of society. As a result of his revolutionary work, Freire was imprisoned and exiled as a subversive by the Brazilian government after the military coup of 1964. After his exile, he first moved to Chile and then emigrated to the United States, later working as an educational consultant at Harvard University. During the 1970s, he worked with the Office of Education of the World Council of Churches in Geneva, Switzerland, and helped emerging nations in Africa and Latin America to develop literacy programs. After twenty-five years of exile, Freire returned to Brazil, where he has served as a professor and education secretary of Sao Paulo, the largest school system in Brazil.

Freire's religious background is Roman Catholic, and he has been influenced by various philosophies, including phenomenology, personalism, existentialism, and Marxism. Freire refers to himself as a Christian humanist and describes his educational philosophy as humanistic. For Freire, humanization is the goal of every valued educational and social activity. The forces of dehumanization, such as those named in chapter 1, are destructive of true human nature and dignity.[3] Freire's educational philosophy embodies the concerns raised by liberation theologians and can be seen as a twentieth-century expression of a Christian humanism that addresses the conditions of Latin America. Freire's work and its implications will be explored in relation to the theological foundation of education, the context and structures of education, the broader purposes of education, and the actual practice of education with people.

The Theological Foundation of Education

A crucial issue confronting the theory and practice of religious education is the relation of theology to religious education. Sara Little outlined five possibilities that present themselves in the discussion of this issue. These include theology as content to be taught; theology as norm; theology as irrelevant; "doing" theology as educating; and education in dialogue with theology. She also points out that no one alternative is "*the* way" to relate education and theology.[4] But given this warning of positing one definitive way, it is still possible to explore the implications of liberation theology for the resolution of this issue. The relation of theology to both religious and theological education is a foundational concern.

The basic concerns and perspectives of liberation theology would discount Little's first three alternatives. Viewing theology as either content or norm would too readily imply the advocacy of banking education against which Freire most explicitly warns. Freire reacted against those forms of education that stressed cognitive content to the exclusion of consideration of either the persons or the context of the educational experience. He appropriately protested against a lopsided configuration of the educational trinity favoring content as conceived in a traditional and imposed way. But content can be expanded to consider both affective and behavioral or life-style content in a critical appropriation of what tradition offers. Whereas Freire avoids the reductionism of traditionalism that stresses the unchanging character of the educational content, he is subject to the diminution of the full breadth of Christian content in focusing upon the context and persons of the educational trinity. This other reductionism is that of radicalism or contextualism.

In addition, a liberation perspective would preclude viewing theology as irrelevant, except in the case in which theology as content and norm is imposed upon others for the purpose of oppression and domination. Liberation theology in its basic commitments seeks to be involved with the pressing issues confronting oppressed persons. Thus, for these initial and immediate concerns, liberation theologians would affirm that "doing" theology is educating and that education must be in dialogue with theology. In addition, liberation theologians would affirm that education focuses on and encourages the processes in which persons become more skilled at using their faith to reflect upon contemporary experience and using their contemporary experience to reflect upon faith, to discern the action of God in history as it is being written, and to examine their own religious conceptions for adequacy in confronting global realities and problems. Norma Thompson discussed this conception of the relation of theology to religious education in her description of the approach that stresses theologizing—"doing" theology as educating.[5] Beyond this general approach though, liberation theologians would stress the nature of "doing" theology in terms of a commitment to the needs of the oppressed and to reflection that is in a dialectical relationship with action that seeks to transform the world. A transformed world can better address the needs of the poor.

Similarly, liberation theologians voice a concern that theology be in dialogue with education. The focus of this dialogue would need to be upon persons' activities in the world with an interest in praxis. Freire defined praxis as "reflection and action upon the world in order to transform it."[6] From this perspective, religious education should seek to foster and inform the task of critical reflection on the personal and corporate practice of faith. Likewise, theology reflects on the practice of religious education and seeks to inform and foster this practice in present and future activity. In this way, an essential dialectical interaction is established between theology and religious education that seeks to enable the actualization of liberation not only within the church but, more importantly, in the world—where Freire's concern was focused. One could also argue that the world is the center of God's love, even to the extent of sending a son (John 3:16).

Thus the dialogue between liberation theology and religious education and the activity of doing theology in educational experiences from a liberationist perspective called for a unique stance and commitment in the historical situation. In other words, it required that sides be taken—to stand with the poor implied standing against the rich. Such a confrontational approach did not allow for compromise or the voicing of alternative perspectives regarding social, political, or economic realities. Taking sides also assumed the epistemological privilege of the poor, contradicting the concept of the universal need of all persons for religious education.

Three Views of Religion

Paulo Freire drew upon theology and religion for some of his basic views of education. He developed three views of religion and compared them with the type of education that each view of religion would foster. In this analysis, he assumed a radical and prophetic stance. The first view, the traditionalist view of religion, stressed life in the world to come and urged people to realize transcendence without confronting and dealing with worldliness.[7] This view opted out of considering the context of education that is an essential element of the educational trinity. Such a view tended to foster a closed society, maintain the status quo, and promote an education that would inevitably be individualistic. It was judged to be content-centered and fostered "banking education." This first view was judged by Freire to be both alienated and alienating. The danger of this reaction by Freire is to discount the important and potentially transformative place of tradition, especially in the Christian faith.

A second view of religion for Freire, the modernizing perspective, changed some of the current oppressive practices, restating some of its doctrinal positions, and was more involved in problems of a social, economic, or political nature. But Freire viewed the measures taken as only half steps, not bringing about the truly radical changes he proposed. This view spoke of a liberating education; but, in doing this, it stressed a change in technique, a change in individuals rather than the drastic changes that were viewed as needed in terms of societal structures and systems. In relation to the educational trinity, Freire judged this second view to show valid concern for persons but to inadequately address what was required in the educational context.

The third view of religion was the prophetic view, and it committed itself to the dominated classes and sought to transform society radically. Education, according to this view, would always be a mode of action meant to change things, a political program for the permanent liberation of people. The realities of implementing such a prophetic educational practice and avoiding new oppressions challenged those who espoused this view. In embracing this third option, Freire is open to an unbalanced and at times exclusive focus upon the context of education. While affirming the importance of transformation of the context of the community and society, Freire's position can at points be judged to be reductionistic in its redefinition of content and its selection of persons. Persons judged to be oppressors are excluded, and the hermeneutical privilege of the poor and oppressed are assumed. The redefinition of Christian content in terms of political, economic, and social categories as proposed by Marxist analysis are also judged to be reductionistic. Such categories are not all there is to human life. The poor, even when liberated in political and economic life, can manifest a spiritual bondage that perpetuates oppressive structures and systems under their leadership. These were Father Ramos's observations, with which I concur.

Using Freire's analyses of the three basic views of religion, liberation theology would necessitate that one affirm a prophetic view of religion with a corresponding commitment to liberating education. From this prophetic view, education is always an effort to understand better that which is concrete. As they focus on it together, the educator-educatee (teacher) and the educatee-educator (student) would be joined in creative active presence. They would be engaged in a clarifying praxis and unveiling structural and systemic realities.[8] If one only used liberation theology as the theological basis for religious education, then by necessity one should affirm a prophetic view of religion and a liberating form of religious and theological education. This form of education has been more readily espoused than actively practiced in many settings, but its actual contours can be clarified in a discussion of the context and structures of education.

The Context and Structures of Education

Assuming the priority given to the context in both Freire's thought and the work of liberation theologians, careful assessment must be given to the structures of educational practice. Rubem Alves wrote in 1969, "I believe that we should leave aside the problem of techniques of education and deal with the problem of context and purpose of theological education."[9] In order to analyze a context, one must consider the structures within which such a liberating education is to occur. This consideration relates to the ubiquitous call for contextualization by theologians of liberation. It also relates to the need to ground religious education within the present-day historical situation that includes social, political, and economic realities. The demand was made to analyze and evaluate the structures within which the educator's task is undertaken.

Existing institutions and programs in both religious and theological education in North America were seen as consciously or unconsciously imperialistic, for they consistently maintained the privileges and power of an elite and perpetuated an attitude of dependence or submission among those viewed as powerless. The students within existing institutions and programs were viewed as being coerced into being socialized and dominated via the educational experience in ways that maintained the position and power of those viewed as knowledgeable, experienced, and powerful. Rather than enabling the empowerment of all persons, educational practice was seen as eliminating any dialogue, negotiation, or confrontation among all participants, except for the maintenance of hierarchical status relationships and authority.

Radical Critics: Their Proposals

Radical critics, such as Freire and Illich, proposed a break from this status quo, a reversal of the system, and a return to the people and local values of each region, nation, culture, and subculture—a trend referred to as contextualization.[10] This approach required an engagement with the historical context with a predisposition to radically change the status quo. The context, judged as oppressive, was the primary object of analysis and focus for transformative energy.

Freire pointed out that one could not discuss religious or theological education other than historically. Churches and seminaries were not abstract entities but were and are institutions, structures involved in history. Therefore, to understand the educational role of seminaries or churches, one had to take into consideration the concrete situation in which they exist. There can be, from this perspective, no neutrality of the churches or seminaries and no neutrality of education. When one insisted on the neutrality of the churches or seminaries in relation to history or to political action, one was viewed as taking a political stance that inevitably favored the power elite against the oppressed masses. Denying one's responsibility to choose sides in the conflict between the powerful and the powerless meant to side with the powerful, not to be neutral. Subjective idealism within society maintained the illusion that people's hearts could be transformed while the social structures that make their hearts sick were left intact and unchanged.[11] Liberation theologians called for the need to address the demonic and oppressive forces that exist in structures and the need to transform these structures or to destroy them. Such an analysis served to polarize persons and to clarify political commitments. The potential problem with this analysis was that realities were often more complex and the nature of conflicts were more varied than just between the rich and poor as suggested by the use of class analysis.

Given the problems of oppression, the pressing need identified by Freire and others was to transform the structure of religious and theological education so that the educational experience could be liberating for all participants. If the church was to fulfill its prophetic function and if those participating in theological education were to function as prophets, then a critical analysis of the social structures in which conflict takes place was required. This meant that seminarians needed a knowledge of sociopolitical science, since this science was viewed as demanding an ideological choice. Neither the limitations of sociopolitical science nor the priority of theology were always named in this advocacy for liberation. Education in a prophetic church was to be an instrument of transforming action, a form of political praxis at the service of permanent human liberation. This was not to happen only in the consciousness of people, but presupposed a radical change of structures in which the consciousness of all participants could be transformed.[12]

Such a need for a prophetic ministry required that both theological and religious education foster the critical analysis of its own structure and other structures within the immediate and global context. Participants in such education needed the opportunity to develop such skills of analysis with ample opportunity for feedback from educators and other educatees. In the emphasis upon a prophetic stance, the complementary need for pastoral ministry was too readily neglected. The other assumption in this perspective was that structural change would result in the transformation of communities and individuals. In this regard, it is important to note Marie Augusta Neal's concern that religious educators teach the skills needed for calling to account governmental and economic officials for their exploitation of the people and for providing reflective space for the people on every occasion to decide how to redress wrongs.[13] The teaching of such skills and the opportunity for reflection and practice of such skills would require a radical departure from the premises and practices of the dominant academic model in theological education. If in fact the current structures and institutions of theological education could actualize a liberating education, the increase of reflective space and the incorporation of critical analysis throughout the educative experience would be needed. As will be evident in chapter 3, more than the advocacy and service stressed by liberationists are required of the Christian church in teaching within a context. The connection of the ministries of advocacy and service to the tasks of proclaiming the Christian story, forming a community inclusive of both poor and rich, and celebrating worship are too easily forgotten in the prophetic stance as advocated by Freire. This will be explored in chapter 3.

Contextualization

Freire called upon religious educators to participate in an ongoing process of mutual empowerment with others such that structures and those responsible within structures were called to account. This process recognized the dynamic of change within each context and stressed the need for contextualization. But with such a stress upon change and even revolution, liberating educators may fail to identify any points of possible continuity with the past and with tradition. The ideal of transcending the past is not always possible or desirable in every situation, recognizing the need for both continuity and change in human life. Opting for revolutionary change may not always result in any significant change in the actual day-to-day life of poor folk if spiritual conversion does not accompany social conversion.

Liberation theologians emphasized the task of contextualization. This task seeks to take very seriously the concrete historical situation in which education and ministry occur. In relation to theology, this implies a concern for incarnation in life. Just as the Child of God became incarnate in the person and work of Jesus of Nazareth, Christians are to incarnate the values of Christ's reign in concrete historical settings. The danger of this emphasis upon contextualization is the preoccupation with one's context to the exclusion of intercontextual or transcontextual realities. Such a preoccupation produces contextualism which identifies all truth with one's individual or communal context to the exclusion of the global and universal connections that transcend immediate and particular local concerns.

Victor Nazario's insights, offered in relation to the third Mandate Programme of the Theological Education Fund, while recognizing the dangers of contextualism helped to discern the positive aspects of contextualization as understood from the perspective of liberation theology. Contextualization was intended to result in definite political commitments and action on behalf of the oppressed. It proposed a radical critique that necessitated the transformation of structures and included the possibility of revolution. It comprised a perspective that negated the very language and conceptions of developed nations and resisted the imposition of their categories on the life experience and reflection of communities in developing nations.[14] Such a wholesale rejection of First-World categories becomes problematic in working for peace and justice on a global scale, but it did provide a space for the autonomy and independence of Third-World people and communities prior to seeking points of interdependence and cooperation.

From the perspective of religious education in the developed nations, the contextualization and concrete rootedness of liberation theology called for a radical critique of historical realities in light of the experience and reflection of Third-World communities. It required observing and critiquing, actively and carefully, the theological and religious education that had bought heavily into the predominant economic, political, and social life of First-World commitments. In this process of reflection and action, the use of social sciences was promoted to analyze situations and especially the use of Marxist understandings to probe the nature and divisiveness of capitalism. However, the naming of capitalism as the enemy by some liberationists did not enable them to adequately critique the highly favored and proposed alternative of socialism. Contextualization in this case succumbs to contextualism and the pursuit of a political agenda without fostering the critique made possible with intercontextual and transcontextual dialogue.

From a First-World perspective, contextualization may be viewed as the dynamic process through which the church continually challenges and/or transforms elements of the cultural and social milieu of which it is an integral part in its daily struggle to realize liberation in its life and mission in the world.[15] A similar challenge is posed for Christians in the developing nations and requires a critique of their context. The critique and possible transformation of any context requires clarity with regard to the purposes of education and the possibility of intercontextual dialogue.

The Purposes of Education

Second in priority to the context of religious education, the question of its purposes was raised by liberationists. Basic issues that probe the nature of these purposes included three following areas. The following areas were named in ecumenical discussions and are related here to the specific field of theological education.

First, what is theological education for? If the task of theological education is seen in terms of expressing the gospel, curriculum and teaching must be such that students are trained to reformulate the gospel in expressions understandable to their communities. If the task of theological education is seen in terms of fulfilling the ministry of the people of God, students must be trained to equip the laity so that they may fulfill their ministry through their daily vocations.

Second, what kind of future leaders are desired for the church? Is the aim to produce women and men to fit easily in the existing structure? Or, perhaps more important still, is the aim to produce women and men who have the conviction, courage, and capacity to change and transform structures and the world? How important is it for future leaders of the church to have a deep compassion toward the poor and the oppressed and to be committed to the gospel of liberation of all people from the bondage of body, soul, and mind?

Third, where and how does one do *theology?* What is the place of existing theological institutions in the training of theologizing? Are such institutions the only training grounds or are there alternatives? Can theology be taught only in classrooms? Mainly by lectures? Can the existing theological institutions be renewed, reformed, and opened up for new patterns in theological education?[16]

These questions probed the broader purposes of theological education. The concerns and conceptions of liberation theologians began to provide clues that were to be contextualized in each unique historical situation. Paulo Freire placed emphasis upon the social and political dimension of religious education from the perspective of the oppressed. The task of religious education for the oppressed would therefore entail fostering their conscientization so that they might corporately become engaged in transforming their world.

The emphasis upon the context of education was subject to the danger of not giving adequate attention to elements of content and people. A consideration of the broader purposes of education requires a balanced reference to all the elements of the educational trinity. In a stable society, a balance among the three elements of content, people, and context may be possible; but, in a revolutionary society, the element of context and its change often looms large. However, once a context is transformed, even by revolution, the challenge remains of sharing transformative content that people can internalize and live out. Transforming the context does not immediately translate into transformed persons who themselves share transformative content with successive generations. A holistic approach is required that recognizes the integral connections of the educational trinity of content, people, and the context of community and society.

The unique character of present-day society includes its global character, which must be balanced with any emphasis upon local contextualization. The preoccupation with contextualization in relation to a multicultural world can result in new forms of ethnocentrism that fail to connect with realities outside of the immediate context or cultural community. In a similar way, the preoccupation with globalization can result in what William A. Dyrness has identified as "xenocentrism," the failure to see any value in the local context or culture while embracing the perspective of the other, the stranger.[17] This is a particular danger for First-World educators enamored with Freire who do not give adequate consideration to the purposes of Christian education. The particular purposes of Christian education will be discussed in chapter 3. These purposes can help Christian educators to discern what insights from Freire's work are appropriate for their context. Along with the foundational questions of theological foundation, context, and purposes, educators must grapple with the actual practice of education with people.

The Practice of Education with People

In terms of pedagogical patterns, the seminaries were viewed by liberationists as having generally failed to serve as a paradigm for church and ministry. Perhaps the most telling problem in relationship to pedagogy was the viability of learning significant substance without simultaneously being engaged in practice and concrete historical action. The design of field education and clinical pastoral experiences attempt to address this concern in the current practice of seminaries. Learning in such settings depends on reflection upon the practice and action in which one is currently engaged, which was identified as "praxis." This concern for praxis focuses upon the continuous dialectic between action and reflection. For liberationists, too often the style and patterns of the seminary did not enable a genuine praxis, and therefore the educational experience in seminaries was not a paradigm for the congregation. One can question whether it *should* be a paradigm. In a real sense, for those advocating change, seminary education had become dysfunctional and perpetuated a banking model of education that increased alienation for students. Theological education was to be realized most fully when students, engaged in ministry, were led into serious study in the traditional disciplines by the issues and needs that arose in their practice. The key concept was *interaction*, relating theory and practice, faith and life, theology and action. The concept of interaction is directly related to the principle of connection I name and is to be affirmed in educational practice.

Given the perceived failure of theological and religious education to center upon praxis, it became necessary to explore other pedagogical models. At this point, the work and writings of Paulo Freire became important for the search of a new pedagogy. But a commitment to praxis did not always address how one could discern true or faithful praxis beyond solidarity with the poor. In addition, the successes of traditional theological education along with its obvious failures were not readily named. History reveals both the lights and shadows of any human endeavor, certainly including efforts in theological education.

Freire's Pedagogical Theory

Freire's clearest description of his pedagogical theory was presented in these words: "Our pedagogy cannot do without a vision of [humanity] and of this world. It formulates a scientific humanist conception that finds its expression in a dialogical praxis in which teachers and learners, together, in the act of analyzing a dehumanizing reality, denounce it while announcing its transformation in the name of the liberation of [humankind]."[18] Freire centered upon praxis as the intersection of reflection and action, and he sought to involve all participants in dialogue. Education was viewed as cultural action for freedom and liberation. In terms of religious education, this social, political, and economic liberation was equated with salvation, as God and God's people actively engaged in history to realize liberation for the oppressed. Freire redefined traditional theological understandings of salvation. Thus, the pedagogy involved a denunciation of oppressive structures and the simultaneous annunciation of structures that enabled the full humanization of people. Using Marxian analysis, this denunciation was that of capitalism and of banking education, which prevented the full participation of all in the educating process as subjects. But even with an espoused liberation perspective, the danger of banking or imposing knowledge persists.

Freire proposed a problem-posing pedagogy. Denis Collins helpfully outlined the content and issues of this pedagogy as follows:

1. There are two stages in liberation that have a fundamental educational quality, and they are (a) educational projects carried on by and with the oppressed before they take power and (b) systematic education in the form of permanent cultural revolution.

2. Authentic pedagogy is undeniably political cultural action.

3. Traditional education employs banking methods that impose knowledge, ideas, values, and curricula.

4. Dialogical education is problem-posing, and educational content that is shared should correspond to the problems of emergent consciousness among participants.

5. Teachers and the expert knowledge of all participants are not excluded from dialogical education.

6. Cultural synthesis is the alternative to cultural invasion.

7. Careful attention to philosophy of education is not a pedagogical luxury but a necessity.[19]

Freire viewed persons as educating themselves by struggling to become free in a historical mode of being and in no other sense. Conditioned as it is by social and political contradictions, education should be a process involving three dialectical moments, including investigation of thinking, thematization (by means of generative words and other codifications), and problematization of social reality. This problematization provoked new moments in the dialectical process. Freire termed these "limit situations" (new comprehensions of reality demanding protest—situations that must be transcended and transformed to accomplish liberation) and "generative themes" (so termed because from investigation and discovery of the people's thematic universe new themes were constantly evoked that again presented themselves as historical reality and tasks to be accomplished in the process of liberation). The process of liberation was never complete, it always demanded new investigation, thematization, and problematization.[20] It was precisely at these points at which traditional religious and theological education were judged to have readily failed in both North and Latin America. As an alternative, Freire proposed new understandings for the content, method, and interpersonal relationships of pedagogical practice.

Content: Liberation and Praxis

The content of religious education from a liberation perspective is to be liberation itself and liberating praxis. Praxis is the point at which reflection and action come together authentically. As Freire has observed, reflection without action is verbalism, and action without reflection is activism.[21] In praxis, the authentic word was to be spoken because it included both reflection and action in an ongoing process. To speak a word apart from praxis was to produce alienation. Therefore, the ideal content focus for liberative education was praxis itself.

Liberation as content meant self-discovery and self-expression, self-determination and self-development. It was a message for the human being that may be conceptualized in words but must also be expressed in corporate action. It represented the basic human need for identity and self-realization, for freedom, equality, and community. The dominant message of educational institutions in the developed nations was viewed as being echoed in religious education: go to school in order to get a better job, in order to earn more money, in order to buy more things. A person was too often merely part of the economic system, a cog in the machinery of production. One's purpose was to produce and consume. The fact that the person may be exploited and learning to exploit was largely ignored.[22] This production and consumption was inherent in what Freire described as "banking education," which presented content as a commodity dispensed to the educated elite by those who were experienced and knowledgeable. But it must be recognized that some sharing of content is necessary and indispensable if any education is to occur. A key distinction is the nature of the sharing and whether the content is imposed or offered with suggestions for alternatives that students may consider. Identification of alternatives can empower the students to make choices and to grapple with their personal and communal commitments that for Freire did not typify banking education. However, my experience in Latin America in some settings that explicitly affirmed a liberation perspective showed that liberation approaches as well as traditional educational approaches can fail to identify content alternatives.

The content-knowledge orientation of theological education was seen to be in opposition to "doing theology," orthodoxy as opposed to orthopraxis.[23] This opposition was too often seen as being irreconcilable without the interlocutor of orthopathos as proposed by Samuel Solivan and named in chapter 1. Doing theology meant the ability to engage in a living dialogue between contemporary issues in faith and obedience and the witness of scripture and tradition. It sought not to find a traditional answer but to be open to the new truth that God was offering a faithful people. This perspective seriously risked the loss of tradition that itself can be transformative. Doing theology was to be the dialogue between faith and life, between theology and practice, between the historical events and the Word of God.[24] In this dialogue, theology was to be realized and orthopraxis embodied in the continuing struggle to realize liberation. In their reaction to traditional content considerations, liberationists may so stress change that any points of continuity are too readily dismissed. But with a totally oppressive context, continuity is not a reasonable option for those on the margin who daily struggle for survival and seek liberation. The social location of those educating and being educated influences the possibility of options.

As Freire suggested, liberation must be considered to be the content of liberative education. Religious and theological educators were to center upon the articulation and realization of liberation within each particular historical context. Such a content orientation implied a utopian perspective in relation to the historical context that too readily ignored the place of continuity while embracing the pressing need for change. This process of liberation was not to be a means of owning or possessing the world or knowledge but a means of transforming the world. Freire used the term "theoretic praxis" to refer to what occurs when one steps back from accomplished praxis, or from praxis that is being accomplished, so as to see it more clearly. But such theoretic praxis was only authentic when it maintained a dialectical movement between itself and a praxis that was carried out in a particular context. Thus, for Freire, the two forms of praxis, theoretic praxis and actualized praxis, were two inseparable moments of the process by which persons reached critical understanding. In other words, reflection is only real when it sends us back to the given situation in which we act.[25] For Freire and others who favored liberation, theological education had often failed to maintain this very dialectic between theoretic praxis and actualized praxis. It did not anticipate specific engagement for liberation from the perspective of liberationists. The academic community was seen as divorced from the larger cultural context where common folk have very practical concerns for survival. But this need not be so. While it must be recognized that far too often this was the case in traditional educational efforts as evaluated by liberationists, alternatives were and are present.

In Freire's writings, one can find implications bearing on the content of religious education. The content is to be drawn primarily from the life of the people: their concerns, problems, fears, and myths. The educator must be careful not to impose ideas on the learners. The content of education was to be found less in books than in the real-life problems of the people. Such a practice of nonimposition as applied to religious education would certainly throw both students and teachers back on their own resources.[26] These resources included the aspirations and strivings for liberation within structures that perpetuated alienation and oppression. Again, the point of departure was to be the concrete historical situation that always served to ground the educational content. The consideration of content must also engage discussion about the actual educational method.

Method: Conscientization

The method of religious and theological education directly affirmed by liberation theologians is *conscientization*. As Freire defined it, conscientization is "learning to perceive social, political, and economic contradictions, and to take action against the oppressive elements of reality."[27]

Elsewhere Freire spoke of conscientization as the development of critical awareness achieved through dialogical educational programs associated with social and political responsibilities.[28] The purpose of this process was to bring about critical attitudes in people; and these critical attitudes, in turn, were to lead to a transformation of the world. From Freire's perspective, this process was the only type of education that respected the true nature of people. A person's God-given freedom was respected in a situation where ideas were not imposed on students but resulted from the open discussion of ideas. This type of education respected the basic equality that should exist among persons in society. The community of people was to be fostered by a type of education in which students and teachers faced each other on an equal basis. The prophetic religion that Freire espoused found as its logical educational component a process in which the ultimate purpose of education was a radical transformation of oppressive social, political, and economic structures.[29]

Freire embraced a full-fledged reconstructionist philosophy of education. Reconstructionism can be affirmed for its critical examination of current social, political, and economic orders and for its concern for social needs. But the terms of this analysis can be questioned. Reconstructionists seriously grapple with human responsibility in the corporate and social realms. They recognize problems in society and see possibilities for radical reform and change. Educators like Freire in this perspective are viewed as primary instruments for social change. Reconstructionists, while recognizing social sins, may ignore the realities of personal sin in the liberators and the oppressed as well as in the oppressors. Their preoccupation with the social order may result in ignoring personal responsibilities, and in their emphasis upon change they may fail to see the need for continuity in personal and corporate life.

Conscientization as a method of theological education involved both denunciation and annunciation. A denunciation of all that is oppressive and alienating in the existing social system was first undertaken. Denunciation was to become a life-giving force leading to liberation, responsible action, and a decisive choice and commitment within history for the oppressed. This denunciation was to be revolutionary and not reformist. Simultaneous with the denunciation of oppression and injustice was the annunciation of liberation and justice. Freire maintained that between denunciation and annunciation was the time for building the historical praxis. For Freire, both denunciation and annunciation could be achieved only in praxis. This method of conscientization was to enable all participants in the educational process to move from a point of neutrality. The intent was not to impose or enforce liberation, because people could only realize their own liberation. This educational method posed the critical questions and enabled participants to consider the alternatives, but it declared the need for commitment and engagement. It posed the questions necessary for engagement and encounter. The freedom in conscientization was for others and not exclusively for oneself. It was for self in community. Persons are bodies-souls-in-community, and liberation themes address them as such. This stress upon the community is to be affirmed to counter the exclusive interest in individuals that characterizes many North American approaches to religious education.

Freire's methods suggested a radical alternative. He proposed a thorough search into the life situation of the students; the choice of themes for discussion to be drawn from the life situation of the people; a graphic representation of these themes; open discussion by all concerned on these themes; and a commitment to action on the part of both students and teacher as a result of discussion.[30] The advocacy of this method poses a challenge to traditional patterns and suggests a way in which to broaden the typical educational agenda. Freire's methods sought to engage people at a different level of relationship. But his opting for the entry point of context within the educational trinity can result in a reductionism that does not adequately address the content and the variety of people, who include oppressed and oppressors of various stripes.

Interpersonal Relationships

The area of interpersonal relationships deals with how teachers choose to be with students. The concern for relationships focuses on the element of persons in the educational trinity. Liberationists called for the mutual recognition of others as persons with worth and dignity. As Freire suggested, a teacher might better be termed an "educator-educatee" because the teacher, while teaching, also is to be open to learning from students. The students are identified as "educatee-educators," recognizing their role in sharing with and teaching others in the educational event. This teaching role is secondary to their role of learning but very much present and recognized. The freedom of students to embrace or question that content shared by teachers was crucial in enabling dialogue to occur. The teacher is to recognize each and every participant in the educational process as a subject and affirm each and every person's dignity and worth and ability to become an active agent in his or her destiny. This affirmation of persons is a very positive aspect of the perspective advocated by Freire. His high view of persons supports a Christian theological anthropology except for the categorical division between the oppressed and oppressors, between the poor and the nonpoor. But Freire's implicit theology has posed a particular challenge in a time of the reappraisal of liberation theology. A reconsideration is required of what may be lost in advocating a radical departure from educational thought and practice with a reconstructionist philosophy.

Reappraisal

Freire's implicit theology represents a redefinition of traditional theological understandings in line with the insights of various liberation theologies. God is seen as the Creator who seeks a relationship of liberation with humanity. God is the active and dynamic God of the Hebrews and the human person of Jesus who acts to save people. God is involved in the ongoing process of creating people and the world with the cooperation of human persons. This cooperative process is one that Freire seeks to replicate in education with teachers and students cooperating to make a difference in the world. Jesus is viewed as the radical critic of oppressive institutions and structures who offers the possibility of redemption and salvation. Redemption is redefined in terms of a Christian's willingness to undergo death by struggling for new life and freedom for oppressed peoples and not remaining neutral in political struggles. Thus sin is viewed as oppression, as it is exercised against persons and by implication against God. Salvation is not viewed so much in terms of individuals as in terms of bringing persons and societies to true freedom (humanization). The Christian gospel is the proclamation of the radical reordering of society in which people are oppressed.[31]

Freire's theology is problematic for those who espouse a more traditional or conservative perspective in the following areas:

> 1. His use of a situational hermeneutic can lead to a distorted interpretation of scripture; political analysis can take priority over biblical theology and distort the biblical message. Freire may not consider scripture as a primary frame of reference.

2. In Freire's theology and philosophy, the absence of the role of the Holy Spirit is apparent. Christ is not mediated through the poor alone, because the demonic can be encountered in the oppressed as well as the oppressors. The Holy Spirit needs to confront the oppressed as well as the oppressors.

3. Freire's anthropologically centered theology does not adequately consider the extent of sin. He essentially views the oppressed as the people of God—not just potentially but actually. But those sinned against are also capable of sin. A transcendent God makes demands upon humanity that extend beyond the call for justice and peace in the economic, political, and social realms.

4. Freire holds to a qualitatively defined and reductionistic view of salvation. Salvation is not automatically appropriated in joining a struggle for liberation, though this may be one expression of the works that flow from faith. An act of faith in God as revealed in Jesus Christ results in works of faith in public as well as private life.

5. In Freire's view, little appreciation exists for the church's role as the proclaimer of the gospel of Jesus Christ. The kerygma is to be proclaimed in word and deed. A full understanding of the church's mission that includes proclamation, community, service, advocacy, and worship is lacking with a focus on service and advocacy in a theology of liberation.

6. A lack of clarity exists in an largely unqualified utopian vision. Hope emerges out of the past and present and must be defined in terms of God's ultimate plans for the creation as revealed in scripture. The place of tradition and its transformative power should not be lost in stressing the future.[32]

In addition, Daniel Schipani, in his analysis of the encounter between liberation theology and religious education, names three problems with the approach of liberation theology. First, this approach overemphasizes the cognitive, verbal, and rational dimensions of understanding to the detriment of the intuitive, emotional, creative, imaginative, and aesthetic dimensions of life. Second, the insistence upon critique and suspicion in reliance upon Marxist and confrontational political analysis may prevent positive engagement in society that includes religious and spiritual responses to conflict. Third, a liberation approach gives little attention to the essential place of tradition and continuity in the Christian faith.[33] With this gap, a liberation approach must be supplemented with other approaches.

In spite of these important criticisms, I can affirm several aspects of Freire's work that challenge North American educators:

1. It addresses the concrete historical situation of people. It is concerned to contextualize education and theology by drawing out the implications of faith and the need for response.

2. It emphasizes a service-oriented salvation and education that are too often ignored.

3. It provides insights for Christian educators in how to educate for social action and how to raise the consciousness of Christians to the realities and needs of people in other cultural contexts.

4. It takes seriously the need to demonstrate an incarnational theology, one that is lived out. It seeks to relate faith to life.

5. It affirms the biblical emphasis upon the poor and oppressed in Christ's ministry (Luke 4:18–19), recognizing the challenges of Marxist ideology.

6. It focuses on the humanity of Christ in reaction to an exclusive emphasis upon his deity.

7. It encourages a critical awareness that the Western World is part of a global problem of oppression and injustice.

8. It emphasizes Christian education as prophetic education, challenging oppressive social structures by (a) questioning those programs and techniques of education that neither consider the social and corporate implica-

tions of the gospel nor question the status quo and (b) developing Christian consciousness of the global context of oppression while leading Christians in constructing new and faithful life-styles.

9. It stresses the need for structural and social transformation to complement a traditional emphasis on personal transformation and redemption in the gospel.

10. It confronts the myth of a life of better "things" and forces an examination of the tension between professed or stated intentions and values (ideas and ideals) and revealed preferences (reality).[34]

Paulo Freire's work and thought can be positively assessed. For example, Schipani identified Freire's contribution as inspiring a religious education that is dialogical in spirit, prophetic-eschatological in vision, praxis-oriented, hermeneutical in character, and communal in shape.[35] This is a major contribution in countering the dominant forms of religious and theological education in North America. The dangers of Freire's perspective emerge when the emphases upon the historical context and the radical equality of people limit the potentially transformative impact that Christian content and traditions can have upon persons, communities, structures, and systems by the grace of God. This can also occur when the wisdom gained by teachers is not shared for fear of imposing content upon students. The sharing of the accumulated wisdom of the faith community and of the wider pursuit of truth does not always equate with banking education. Freire's educational approach can be banked as well as any other educational philosophy and can therefore be subject to the possible reductionisms named in this chapter.

Conclusion

Freire has stated that truly liberating education can only be put into practice outside the ordinary system. This is so because a power elite would not encourage a type of education that denounces them even more clearly than do all the contradictions of their power structures.[36] Given this situation, it is necessary to explore and consider alternatives to theological education as offered in seminary education. The situation in certain church settings may provide more openness. Yet the problem common to both seminaries and churches is the need to explore areas that are free for active reflection and education for critical consciousness.

Can a theology of liberation and its educational model ever be institutionalized? The prophetic stand takes precedence over the institutional forms in this theology. There are paratheological institutional factors that must be explored. They include the following: a close link between certain popular and political movements and the emergence of the theology of liberation for common folk; studies in social science, often outside seminary circles, to expose the contradictions of class and international relationships in the world; independent research by individuals or very small groups with freedom from academic and scholastic norms, which can be an appropriate condition for creative intellectual integrity; and encounters of regional, national, and global leaders to develop strategies for liberating action. Christians should not invest all hopes in formal theological education schemes to accomplish change.[37] Some other alternatives include:study centers, lay training centers, urban industrial mission and training centers, theological education by extension, decentralized training programs, clinical pastoral education, community development programs, local community-based theological training, base communities and cells, ad hoc educational events, and opportunities for theological reflection on liberation movements themselves.[38] All of these alternatives need to be explored and related to the general effort of theological education in concrete ways. Historically, these alternatives have also survived in relationship with traditional forms. Such traditional forms, although they have been criticized, have been drawn upon by those advocating liberation in theology and education.

Both traditional educational forms and those advocated by Freire grapple with Christian disciples' calling to teach the gospel in the world. All that Jesus commanded is to be taught, and his disciples are called to obey his teachings (Matt. 28:20). Freire wrestles with the implications of Christian discipleship in Latin America and throughout the world. A similar challenge awaits all who seek to follow Christ in their ministry of teaching.

The exploration of the implications of liberation theologies and especially the work of Paulo Freire for religious and theological education points up the need for a more comprehensive vision for education to include key insights and challenges while affirming the place of continuity and traditions that can transform current realities. The proposal of such a comprehensive vision is the focus of chapter 3, which proposes a model for transformative Christian education. Religious educators in North America can gain much through critical interaction with liberation educators such as Paulo Freire. Without this interaction a faithful response to global realities is not possible today.

Transformative
Christian Education

In the light of the challenges posed by liberation theologies, Christians in North America are called upon to consider the possibility of change for a vast host of people to the south. Christians have affirmed the possibility of transformation as persons and communities enter a living relationship with God that impacts upon all of life.[1] Transformation in general can be defined as the process of going beyond existing or dominant forms to a new or emergent perspective and reality. Going beyond is of greater interest if one is positioned on the margin, as is the case of the poor in Latin America and of Christians who seek an alternative to oppressive communal and societal norms in any setting. The need for this transformation has been evident in Latin America as Christians have called for the liberation made possible in Jesus Christ that leads to a new form of personal and corporate life. But transformation is also an option for North American Christians as they respond to realities in North America and throughout the world. One North American Hispanic, David Abalos, views transformation as "the creation of alternatives that present new and better possibilities for all of human life."[2] The need for alternatives is apparent in seeing how the destroyers of life have ravaged many people in Latin America.

Historically, among Christian communities, this interest in transformation has primarily but not exclusively focused on the individual response of people to the call of Jesus Christ and their faith in the provision of salvation offered in his person and work. By embracing this salvation, people are able to experience a new way of life as embodied in the Christian faith, which asserts that only by the grace of God can people respond to the gifts of salvation and their adoption into the very family of God with all of the resulting privileges and responsibilities. While this emphasis upon personal transformation is to be celebrated in a time when personal accountability and integrity are viewed as secondary concerns in U.S. society, it can too readily neglect a comprehensive appreciation of the breadth and depth of Christian transformation or conversion that is present in both personal and corporate life.[3] With a view to widening and deepening our appreciation of the full dimensions of Christian faith, Christian educators must consider the nature and implications of transformation or conversion in their ministries. The term "Christian educators" refers to all Christians, clergy and laity, who educate both explicitly and implicitly through their lives and actions. In order to begin this consideration, Christian educators must first explore the biblical foundation of conversion which is central to understanding transformation within a Christian tradition.

A Biblical Foundation

As John Marsh points out, in biblical usage, "conversion" refers to the act of turning or returning. In the Hebrew scriptures, the term *sub*, which means to turn back, can refer to God's turning to people either favorably (as in Deut. 13: 17, where God is described as "turning" from anger to mercy and compassion) or negatively (as in Josh. 24:20, where the nation of Israel is warned that if they forsake God and serve foreign gods, God will "turn" from them). "Conversion" also refers to persons turning back to (*sub*) God (as in the case of Jer. 3:14, where persons respond to God's choice) or away from God (as in the case of Jer. 8:4-6, where persons are turning away and pursuing their own course in life). In general, the turning of persons *from* God is viewed as rebellion, whereas persons turning *to* God is viewed as the work of God's grace and human cooperation with it. This turning to God is "more than a change of mind, more than undergoing some experience; it is a concrete change to a new way of life."[4] That new way of life provides an alternative to the realities experienced by the vast host of people in Latin America as described in chapter 1.

In the New Testament, the followers of Jesus were described as followers of "The Way" as a result of their conversions. Christians were people who had turned from (*epistrepho*) a former way of living to embrace a new way in Jesus Christ. But it is important to note that the New Testament, as Marsh indicates, does not speak of God's turning to people. This is the case because the incarnation itself is the fulfillment of all such turning on the part of God to encounter people. God turns to humanity through the incarnation of the second person of the Trinity. Though conversion is used to describe the act of turning away from (*epistrepho*), as in Gal. 4:9, it is most often used for people turning to God (Acts 9:35; 15:19). True turning to God follows upon the three experiences of repentance, belief, and faith. *Repentance* is the turning from sin, from separation from God and involves a change of mind and a corresponding feeling of remorse or regret for one's past disobedience. Repentance ushers people into a new way of life. *Belief* is the content of what people affirm about God and the human condition in relation to God. Belief explores an understanding of how God wants people to live and to live together. *Faith* focuses upon with whom one walks and, in conversion, leads not only to a new way of life for the person of faith but to a fundamental spiritual transformation as well.[5]

One question that has been raised in relation to conversion from New Testament sources is whether radical or gradual conversion is in view. A decision with regard to this issue will influence one's philosophy of and approach to Christian education in relation to conversion. The so-called Pauline paradigm, as described by *Lukan* sources in Acts 9:1–19; 22:1–21; and 26:1–23, emphasizes conversion as an event that is radical and life-transforming in nature. This Pauline paradigm has been stressed in evangelism and evangelization, but a careful consideration of Paul's conversion suggests that even he gained a fuller experience of his conversion only over time (Gal. 1:15–19).

A distinct paradigm that has not received as much interest is what can be termed the "Petrine" or "Markan" paradigm for conversion. Peter's conversion can be viewed as a process that began with his confession near the town of Caesarea Phillipi that Jesus was the Messiah, recorded in Matt. 16:13–19. As C. Ellis Nelson observes, "Peter was the first disciple to understand the divine mission of Jesus, and to whatever extent we can say a person is saved when making a confession, Peter is that person."[6] This same Peter was used mightily by God in preaching on the day of Pentecost, and yet he was not thoroughly converted because his understanding of the gospel did not include a place for the Gentiles. This awareness of a more thorough and radical conversion is revealed in the tenth chapter of Acts, where Peter is confronted by God and Cornelius to embrace a new dimension of the gospel, of which he was previously unaware. Peter's conversion, in the Lukan interpretation, occurred in baptizing the first Gentile convert to the Christian faith to a more inclusive understanding of the Christian community. This second conversion directly correlates with the second task of the church, which will be discussed below. Nelson points out that Peter was already converted under the teaching of Jesus and that he was the human founder and recognized leader of the church; yet not all areas of his inner self were converted. Peter had been formed as a Jew, and this early training which precluded equality with Gentiles remained after his conversion at Caesarea Phillipi. It required a unique second encounter with God to break the formation of Peter's youth and to transform his mind so that he could see the gospel in a new light that he had not previously discerned.[7]

In an analysis similar to Nelson's, Richard Peace proposes in his dissertation, "The Conversion of the Twelve: A Study of the Process of Conversion in the New Testament," that the unifying theme in the Gospel of Mark is the unfolding conversion of the twelve apostles as they discover, stage by stage, who Jesus is. He argues that this paradigm of conversion as a process must be given equal weight with the Pauline paradigm of conversion as an event.[8] Thus biblical warrant exists for a broader understanding of conversion that can include both radical and gradual elements of transformations as people encounter God. The Reformed theologian Herman Bavinck came to affirm this broader understanding of conversion when he maintained that a Christian needs two conversions: one away from the world to Jesus Christ, the other in the name of Christ back to the world.[9] This chapter argues the case for multiple conversions where these transformations or turnings relate to the five distinct tasks of the Christian church. Such a broadened understanding of conversion is also warranted on the basis of the actual accounts of persons who have experienced conversion in their lives.[10] It may also be possible to argue for the case of continual conversion beyond the naming of multiple conversions in the life of faith that are centered on the five tasks of the church named below.

In summarizing the insights gained from the biblical concept of conversion, Orlando Costas, a missiologist who had a significant ministry in Latin America, made the following five observations:

> First, conversion means a turning from sin (and self) to God (and God's work). Second, this act involves a change of mind, which implies the abandonment of an old world view and the adoption of a new one. Third, conversion entails a new allegiance, a new trust, and a new life commitment. Fourth, conversion is but the beginning of a new journey and carries implicitly the seed of new turns. Fifth, conversion is surrounded by the redemptive love of God as revealed in Jesus Christ and witnessed to by the Holy Spirit.[11]

Conversion thus suggests a radical reorientation for people that requires the centering of all of life upon the will and reign of God. God's reign embraces not only the personal dimension of life but also the communal and societal dimensions whose effects may not be as readily discerned and addressed. Historically, Christian communities have tended to stress either the personal or corporate dimensions of conversion, but both are essential along with a lifelong openness to new turnings. Conversion implies that a center for life exists in the triune God and that people at every point in their lives are moving in ways that are either directed toward that center or away from it. Therefore, it is possible to conceive that a person who has been "converted" at some earlier point in life may now actually be moving in directions that center not upon God but away from God. Likewise, it is possible to conceive of a person who has not been "converted," as perceived by the Christian community, as moving in a direction that *is* centered upon God. This possibility has been theologically designated "prevenient grace" to describe the work of God and the response of people prior to the point of one's conscious and public conversion.

A similar analysis can be suggested for both communities and societies and is certainly warranted in the light of the teaching of Matt. 25:31-46, where judgment focuses on the works of nations and not individuals, and in the light of the teaching of Rev. 2 and 3, where judgment focuses on the works of various Christian communities or churches. Both nations and local communities are evaluated on the basis of the direction of their lives and actions, as either being centered on God or being centered upon other gods. The apostle Paul described this choice to the Christians at Rome as between worshipping and serving the Creator or worshipping and serving created things (Rom. 1:25). Thus a constant choice is posed for societies, communities, and individuals as to whether they will center their lives upon God and choose life or center their lives upon idols and choose death. Modern sensitivities grate at seeing life in such terms, but such a stance was not uncommon to the prophetic tradition found in the Scriptures. This stance does not negate the existence of the many complex areas of our lives where the choices between life and death are not readily apparent or easily resolved. But it does affirm the need to struggle with how our personal and corporate lives embody and/or deny the reality of our conversion, the reality of our turning to God in response to the grace revealed in Jesus the Christ. This stance also affirms the need of Christian educators to assess their efforts in relation to the radical demands of Christian conversion to embrace all of life. In order to address this challenge, educators must name and claim a vision that comprises a comprehensive understanding of transformation and holds forth the possibility of new turnings in the walk of faith.

A Comprehensive Vision for Transformation

Building upon a biblical concept of conversion, Christian educators must be able to conceive of Christian education in a way that links theory and practice to the primary tasks of the church. Without such a linkage, any discussion of transformation remains just an intellectual exercise and Christian education remains undistinguishable from education in general. In the effort to explore a linkage, I would like to propose the following working definition of Christian education and to suggest its implications in relation to one model for the tasks of the church.

Christian education can be defined as the process of sharing or gaining the particulars of the Christian story and truth (information) and Christian values, attitudes, and life-style (formation) and fostering the conversion of people, communities, societies, and structures (transformation) by the power of the Holy Spirit to a fuller expression of God's reign in Jesus Christ. Education in general can be defined as the process of sharing content with people in the context of their community and society. This process in Christian education requires the partnership of God with people who are called and gifted to teach and the openness of people to the possibility of transformation. This definition incorporates the three essential elements or foci of education that various philosophies of education have stressed: namely, content or information; people or formation; and community/society or transformation.[12]

A comprehensive vision of Christian education would seek to elaborate upon this "educational trinity" of content, people, and community/society, recognizing that in education people are taught content in the context of their community and society. An exclusive emphasis on one or even two of these elements does not foster a comprehensive vision and can result in a truncated practice. The history of educational thought and practice reveals that advocates have often stressed one or two of these elements out of proportion to their relative importance, resulting in limited possibilities for participants and an inappropriate reductionism. From the perspective of embracing the whole counsel of God, such reductionistic efforts in the Christian church have not been faithful and have promoted an educational idolatry. The quality of education resulting from a less-than-comprehensive vision can impact the life of a community and society for generations, as evidenced by the history of Christian education.[13]

The educational trinity is related to the theological understanding of orthodoxy, orthopraxis, and orthopathos proposed by Solivan and discussed in chapter 1. The concern for orthodoxy incarnates an interest in true content or thought. The concern for orthopraxis incarnates an interest in true living or action in the context of the community and society. The concern for orthopathos incarnates an interest in true passion or desire that people embrace as they reflect the passions and desires upon the very heart of God through their lives and ministries.

A similar danger is present for those educators who do not relate their efforts of teaching and learning to the five principal tasks of the Christian church and the corresponding forms of conversion. These five principal tasks serve to distinguish Christian education from education in general. This analysis also suggests that pastors must assume their responsibilities as teachers, as religious educators in their congregations, and support the efforts of others in the congregation that have gifts for teaching. This responsibility is expected of all those who would serve as leaders in the church who are described as being "apt or able to teach" (1 Tim. 3:2; 2 Tim. 2:24).[14]

It is possible to envision the five principal tasks of the church in terms of a web or network. This web can be drawn as a circle or mandala with four points or tasks on the circle's perimeter and with the fifth task as the hub or center. The four tasks on the circle include those of call and commitment (*kerygma*), community and covenant (*koinonia*), care and concern (*diakonia*), and conscience and challenge (*propheteia*). At the center is the fifth task, celebration and creativity (*leitourgia*). Other terms that can be applied to these five tasks are proclamation, community, service, advocacy, and worship.[15] The metaphor of a web suggests that these five tasks must be intimately connected if a full understanding, appreciation, and expression of conversion is to be nurtured in the educational ministry of the church. In relation to each of the points on the web, Christian people can experience conversion, and efforts of Christian education can foster the possibilities for such experiences. This model does not suggest that Christian educators can effectuate conversion, which is the work only of God through the Holy Spirit in the lives of people, communities, and societies. But it does suggest that those called and equipped to teach share the full implications of conversion for life under God's reign. How that teaching is emphasized is very much dependent upon the context of the United States as compared with Latin America. But before considering the United States, the theological connections of the five-task model must be mentioned.

As with the educational trinity, these five tasks are related to the theological interplay or dance of orthodoxy, orthopraxis, and orthopathos. *Kerygma* is an expression of the interest in orthodoxy for true teaching that people are called upon to affirm and embrace. *Koinonia* and *diakonia* are expressions of the interest in orthopraxis for true community and true service respectively. *Propheteia* and *leitourgia* are expressions of the interest in orthopathos for true passion and worship. In the case of *propheteia,* true passion and desire are viewed in terms of God's reign with the embracing of suffering and the compassionate response of advocacy. In the case of *leitourgia,* true worship is viewed in terms of embracing God's revelation with reverence, awe, and joy. The Christian faith affirms the possibility of joy in the midst of suffering.

The United States

In contrast with Latin America, the primary dilemma in the United States confronting Christian people who are working for the values of God's reign is that of fragmentation—the lack of meaning of particulars and the whole of life. Fragmentation isolates people from experiencing the wholeness of life intended by God. This fragmentation can be as devastating as the daily encounter with the destroyers of life in Latin America named in chapter 1. Some of these destroyers are confronted by people and communities in the United Sates on a separate scale. But the issue of survival is cast in different terms. One Latin American author, Carlos Fuentes, has described his context as one that struggles with the abundance with poverty, whereas the North American context struggles with the poverty of abundance. Exceptions can be cited to this general observation concerning the Americas; nevertheless, the comparison is insightful.

Many forces operate in U.S. society, with its relative abundance, to isolate or ghettoize the efforts of Christian religious education from the diverse ministries of the Christian community and from the pressing issues of modern life in a highly technological urban society. In the light of this challenge, the foundational need is to clarify a vision of Christian education that emphasizes points of continuity and builds connections for people across the various dimensions of their lives, both locally and globally. This vision and its implementation would enable people to consider the ecology of life that connects the realities of North and South Americans as just one example of the global web of interaction. This web of interaction exists as a consequence of the creation and suggests the need for interdependence.

In addressing fragmentation, it is possible to explore alternatives in Christian education in relation to the web or network described above. In this web, the task of educating in faith is not viewed as a se   it rather as one that is intimately connected with the   s and focused upon the integration of personal and corpor.   . n relation to God's reign and purposes. The educational task is thus primarily one of integration that enables people to see, to understand, and to live out the connection of God, people, and the entirety of creation. Connection must undergird the five tasks named below and must represent a partnership of those committed to and involved in God's mission in the world, which includes proclamation, community, service, advocacy, and worship.

Proclamation

One major task in the ministries of Christian education is that of sharing the Christian story and enabling others to appropriate that story in relation to their lives. In the proclamation of what is true about God, people, and the world, Christians must emphasize the place of choice, commitment, and a personal response to the call of God. Knowing God in a biblical sense engaged a head, heart, and hand response to the good news declared by God and God's spokespersons. In this knowing, occasioned by the proclamation of the gospel, people were willing to stake their lives on the new life offered to them in Jesus Christ. José Miguez Bonino has said that the goal of sharing the Christian faith is not intelligence—not knowing in a cognitive sense alone—but in faithful obedience to the will of God.[16] In relation to *kerygma,* the task is to foster an obedient response to all that Jesus taught as suggested in Matt. 28:18–20. This is a life-long task.

From this perspective, Christian education is a matter of choice and commitment, where people are confronted with God's view of the human situation and the clear, definite call to repent and be converted (Mark 1:15; Acts 2:38, 39). This call to conversion is issued on the basis of the work of Jesus Christ and the gift of salvation offered to those who respond in faith. Such an offer is based upon the grace of God but demands a new life to be lived in allegiance to God's will for all of creation. The initial turning to God in response to Jesus Christ has traditionally been termed "conversion," but what is implied is a predisposition to additional turnings that may be required and in fact anticipated in beginning a new journey with God. The educational task in relation to *kerygma* is to share the information about God, Jesus Christ, and our human dilemma necessary for people to grasp what is both offered to them and demanded of them in issuing a call to conversion. What is offered is a new life, and what is demanded is the willingness to die to one's old life while embracing the new life offered in Jesus Christ. In Latin America, this is evidenced in the place of passionate commitment that responds to the call, the invitation to become God's daughters and sons within a society that through its destructive expressions, through its destroyers, denies Christian values and the gift of life itself. The good news of the *kerygma* stands in contrast with the messages sounded by society in relation to one's survival and possibilities for the present and future.

Community

The issue of conversion embodied in the task of *koinonia* is the turning from a life centered upon oneself or upon one's family or group to a life that is now centered upon a community defined in terms that break all barriers normally associated with a divided humanity. As the apostle Paul declared in Gal. 3:28: "There is no longer Jew or Greek, there is no longer slave or free, there is no longer male or female; for all of you are one in Christ Jesus." With Christ there is no longer any place for the religious, cultural, linguistic, gender, and social distinctions that have served to alienate and divide people, communities, and societies. The nature of community now redefined in Christ affirms the worth and dignity of every person. The promise for all people, whatever their background or standing, is the possibility of being joined to a new community of God, namely the Christian church.

Examples of those who came to appreciate this new understanding of community include the apostles Peter and Paul. As mentioned above, Peter came to embrace a Gentile, Cornelius, as a fellow member of the body of Christ and as a brother with full rights and standing in the community of faith. Paul, as an apostle to the Gentiles, also came to embrace an understanding of slaves that required their masters to treat them as brothers and sisters in Christ, as evidenced in the New Testament book of Philemon. The barrier between slave and free was broken in this new perspective, as was eventually the institution of slavery itself, as Christians came to see the radical implications of what Christ had accomplished. These examples of Paul and Peter are all the more remarkable in light of the fact that the first-century Jewish male would regularly give thanks to God in worship that he was not born a Gentile or a woman. In addition, Jews of the first century had much contempt for slavery. What this then suggests is that both Peter and Paul were converted from their previous, exclusive understanding of community to embrace a new covenant of grace that was inclusive of all people who placed their faith in Jesus Christ. This new covenant implied that the Christian community was to be characterized by diversity with a unity rooted in Jesus Christ.

Much attention has been given to the rise in Latin America of home Bible studies, house churches, and base ecclesial communities, or basic Christian communities that represent a new form of church in terms of the brotherhood and sisterhood they foster among small groups of people, many of whom are poor. This development represents a shift from a church *for* the poor to a church *with* the poor and *of* the poor. The challenge posed for the church in North America in relation to such renewed understandings and experiences of community is to go about the task of fostering interdependence among people in a way that is specific to a locale but not parochial in its outlook. A false sense of community can lead to acquiescence in the face of suffering that does not move onto an outlook of hope and constructive action for change. Community must be understood in relation to opting for the poor and for people of various economic and social standings whose identity is based upon a relationship with the resurrected Christ.

The emergence of new communities in Latin America poses the question of human and Christian solidarity in response to suffering, alienation, and death, experienced in a multitude of forms. This suffering is an expression of the sin that plagues human existence in the personal and corporate dimensions of life. Sin is a deeply rooted problem that requires the radical transformation offered in Christ. This transformation finds expression in the life and ministry of the Christian community as it engages the world. What this suggests for Christians in North America is the willingness to be touched and moved to action by the suffering experienced by others in our midst and by the strangers and aliens who are present in our society in increasing numbers. This sensitivity is to parallel any concern for those who suffer in Latin America. These people must be embraced as members of the human community and actual or potential members of the redeemed community of the Christian church. This also suggests that the strength of a community is revealed in its willingness to accept those who are viewed as different or those who have been historically excluded from the community because of their race, ethnic background, gender, or socioeconomic status.

In our time, the struggle of women and others to gain their full privileges in the Christian community points out the need to see conversion as a continual process in the life of the church and society. The educational task in relation to *koinonia* is the fostering of a sense of community that implies the formation of people throughout their life span for a life of interdependence with God, with other Christians in their global and local expressions, with humanity in its amazing religious plurality, and with the entire creation. Such a perspective embraces a conversion from the numerous parochial and tribal associations that characterize communal and societal life to a cosmic and universal appreciation of the Christian community.

Given the multiple divisions that plague the global community, the conversion suggested for this task of *koinonia* is no less radical than that related to *kerygma*. Today, as in the first century, there is to be neither black nor white in South Africa or the United States, neither Catholic nor Protestant in Northern Ireland, neither Sandinista nor Contra in Nicaragua—anywhere Christians gather and where such distinctions undermine an essential unity. How is this possible? It is one of the marvels of the Christian faith to overcome the distance between people, communities, and societies. It necessitates a conversion that works toward justice for all of humanity.

Personally, I had a glimpse of what such a conversion to *koinonia* embodies when I went fishing one day with my father and son at Canarsie Pier in Brooklyn, New York. People were fishing together that day from every racial, ethnic, and cultural group represented in the city of New York. Women and men, girls and boys of all ages were fishing, and a sense of harmony and community existed among those people assembled on that hot, sundrenched summer day. Everyone shared in the activity and enjoyment of fishing. People shared their bait, their advice, their stories, and even themselves in an amazing way. This was just one small picture of what Jesus intended for his followers and what God intends for those called into the new reign of Jesus Christ.

Service
Diakonia embodies the answer to the question: "For what purpose are people converted?" In an ultimate sense that question is

answered in terms of glorifying and enjoying God forever. But in a penultimate sense, that question is answered in terms of the care and concern of the whole people of God for the needs of persons, societies, and the world. This task requires that all Christians identify with a pastoral calling not limited to the professional clergy but including the laity in various expressions of mission and ministry.

In Latin America, the meaning of pastoral care and service embraces the response of the whole people of God to the needs of people, society, and the world. All Christians can identify with a pastoral calling that has moved beyond the domain of the professional clergy to include the laity in the various expressions of mission and ministry. This has been a particular focus for people in the house churches and base ecclesial communities who may not have had available to them the services of clergy and yet who must respond to the pastoral needs of their setting. Especially impressive to me were the expressions of sacrificial giving and service I witnessed repeatedly in Central America that people of very limited resources demonstrated in response to human need.

One example of this expression was the response of Christians in Costa Rica to the victims of Hurricane Joan in 1988, in which the Nicaraguan towns of Bluefields and Corn Island were devastated. This response was remarkable because of the animosity that has existed historically between these two Central American republics, exacerbated by the drain of very limited resources to meet the needs of Nicaraguans in Costa Rica. Nicaraguans constitute roughly 10 percent of the Costa Rican population and have been viewed by many as the Samaritans in their midst. A comparable challenge for the Christian community in the United States is its response to persons with AIDS, who have assumed the status of modern-day Samaritans in U.S. society. In broader terms, the issue for religious educators is exploring the connection between one's faith and faithful acts of service. A choice we confront in the United States is whether those who have *received* care in the past will accept their responsibility for those who *need* care today through adequate support of education. This is a particular challenge when the children and youth in need of education belong to a different racial or ethnic group from the majority of taxpayers.

The educational task in relation to *diakonia* is fostering the connection of one's faith to faithful acts of service, the connection between faith and life in the marketplace and community. Christians must understand that knowledge of the Christian faith implies a willingness and predisposition to serve in whatever capacity is needed in response to overwhelming needs that exist at every level of society. Yet what becomes apparent in our current global situation is that the needs of the poor are increasingly aggravated with a widening gap between the rich and the poor. This situation requires Christians seriously and conscientiously to consider responding to the call to serve by opting for the poor. Such an option does not exclude the need for ministry at all socioeconomic levels but poses the question of priority in the allocation of increasingly limited resources. Exposure to realities in the Third World can provide the occasion for conversion to a new commitment in relation to Christian service. But even in the United States a decision is called for today as to whether care will be provided to those currently in need. Such a choice is posed in relation to resources designated for all forms of education and especially child care in the United States.

One example of how a program in Christian education can be "turned" around in relation to the task of service or *diakonia* comes from an adult Sunday school class of working-class folk that was held in a local church in Massachusetts.[17] Class members decided that their weekly discussion of the Christian faith required some joint expression of service. A decision was made to hold monthly "barn-raising" events in which class members, their families, and any other interested persons could participate in various ways in a work project on one Saturday of each month. The projects identified included the repair of a roof that required a team effort, the cleaning out of an attic and cellar for an older adult who could not do the work, the repair of rooms needed to shelter battered women and their children, and the disposal of refuse from an inner-city facility for the homeless which could not be done by its staff. Persons were free to participate in whatever capacity their time and abilities allowed. Each work project was followed up with a potluck dinner, dessert, and a time for singing, socializing, and prayer. Persons who could not do the work were welcome to the dinner, dessert, or social time. Through the experience of service together in various work projects, this initially loosely associated group of adults became a closely knit group that addressed important issues of their faith when they gathered for Sunday school and reflected upon their experiences of serving others. This class experienced a conversion in relating their faith to concrete needs within their community that otherwise would not have been addressed. Class members also experienced a conversion in relationship to an activist style of life, witnessed to by deeds as well as by words, which is called for by the gospel.

Advocacy

The prophetic task of the church is one that has not been as readily owned or nurtured in recent U.S. history as in recent developments in Latin America. What this suggests is that the Christian church in the United States has too readily accommodated the faith to the dominant culture and that Christians have assimilated to a highly materialistic and individualized life-style. This accommodation is also a danger in socialist countries such as Nicaragua and Cuba with a stress on a predetermined corporate agenda that neglects individual freedoms and eliminates vocal dissent. An emphasis upon prophecy and advocacy is the task explicitly named for the church in relation to *propheteia*. Therefore, one can conclude that the Christian church in the United States needs to be converted in embracing this task that some in Latin America have modeled. This is the case because the gospel affirms the place of denunciation as well as annunciation. The cry for justice and human rights heard from those inside and outside of the borders of the United States can be seen as a challenge for Christians to express their social love in the world by advocating for those who are oppressed. In the United States, the ethics of inadequately supporting general education and Christian education must be examined with reference to the development of our greatest resource—people, who are created in the very image of God and who deserve care.

The prophetic task of the church is very apparent in various ministries throughout Latin America with an impact upon educational priorities. The cry for justice and human rights is an expression of Christians' social love in the world. In both Costa Rica and Ecuador, between 25 and 30 percent of the national budgets are designated for education. In the United States, we must see the link between national priorities and the place of education in our communities and lives. We must see the link between denominational priorities and the place of religious education in our churches. A stance of advocacy assumes that we recognize the political dimensions of education in terms of the persons and communities that are being formed in a society. To do otherwise is to deny our prophetic calling.

.sk in relation to *propheteia* is the raising of the
people to the see what the full implications of a
commitment to God's reign mean in relation to the dominant virtues and ideals of one's community or society. Advocacy and orthopathos arise from the whole-hearted embrace of the values, virtues, and ideals of God's reign in the world. Points of convergence or complementarity between gospel values, virtues, and ideals and those of one's culture are to be celebrated and conserved. However, points of divergence and conflict require of Christians a stance of protest and a willingness to struggle with the possibility of transformation or conversion. It can be claimed that Christians have their first allegiance to the Christian faith and that in relation to *propheteia* they are people of hope who are willing to stake their lives on the changes God can bring to fruition in the culture of their society. These changes require the work of the Holy Spirit at all levels of personal and corporate life and the willingness of Christians to accept their responsibilities as being *in* but not *of* the world.

The conversion suggested in this prophetic task of the church entails risk and vulnerability as evidenced by those who assumed the mantle of prophet in the Hebrew scriptures. But to shun this task is to deny the prophethood of all believers which is implied in the ministry of reconciliation given to Christians (2 Cor. 5:16–21). Christians are called to be about the task of reconciling their personal and corporate world to God, which requires holding forth the possibility of conversion, of turning where it is needed. Conversion implies the denunciation of former realities where they are not faithful to God and the annunciation of new possibilities in Jesus Christ that embrace the totality of creation. The prophets of old assumed this task of calling peoples and nations to account before God, and Christians today must not shrink from such a demand.

Worship

The final tasks of the church which mark its distinctive role now and through eternity are those of worship, celebration, and the expression of creativity that gives glory to God. These tasks are placed at the center or hub of the circle in my model to designate their priority and the potentially integrative role that worship can have in the church. In relation to worship, people can experience the joy that God intends for all of creation through the redemption made possible in Jesus Christ and the presence of the Holy Spirit. Such an experience, though heightened in corporate worship, is not limited to that occasion. A sense of worship and of God's presence can encompass all of life, even when only two or three are gathered in the name of Jesus.

One distinctive aspect of Latin American culture is the role of celebration in adding a sense of joy and spontaneity to all of life, even in the midst of the destroyers of life. Through celebration, Latins Americans are able to affirm their Christian hope, which is often a hope that stands against human possibilities and in the face of suffering. In fiesta, the gift of life itself is celebrated and a better future is anticipated. An issue for Christian educators to pose to their communities is: What has happened to the joy?

Much of life in this world forces people to have a preoccupation with all that is created, with little or no time held sacred for an interest in the Creator. This preoccupation is only broken when people choose to come apart. The act of coming apart does not presume a relocation of people from the midst of everyday activities, demands, and contexts. But it does require a willingness to encounter God in the ordinary affairs and interactions of life. Yet in order to gain such an appreciation, people do need to have a place for sabbath in their lives, where the designation of sacred time and space signals an openness to be recreated and refreshed by God's grace in subsequent conversions. It also signals the affirmation that people are created by God and in being created in God's image are created creative. Here then is the possibility of people being empowered by God to use their diverse creative abilities and energies for the glory of God.

The educational task in relation to *leitourgia* is fostering a sense of worship to encompass all of life and exploring avenues for integration that are afforded people through creative expression. Opportunities for the expression of the creativity of all participants in an educational program foster the sense of celebration and provide occasions for worship. In addition, a conversion is implied in enabling people to incorporate the place of sabbath in their personal and corporate lives where the demands of life can be seen in a new perspective—the perspective of a recreated life in Christ.

Conclusion

This chapter has argued for an understanding of conversion that is multiple in character and comprehensive in scope. Orlando Costas has aptly observed that conversion requires new turnings throughout one's life because conversion continues to be needed until the consummation of God's reign.[18] This multiple character of conversion embraces all the dimensions of personal and corporate life with a new way, a new perspective instituted in Christ. The comprehensive scope of conversion impacts upon the five tasks of the church: proclamation, community, service, advocacy, and worship.

As a result of this understanding of transformation, Christian educators are challenged to relate their efforts to the possibility of conversion throughout the life span of people, communities, and societies. They are also challenged to reflect the ongoing nature of conversion itself in their own theory and practice. With such a challenge in mind, Bernard Lonergan, a Roman Catholic theologian, has described conversion as three dimensional:

It is intellectual inasmuch as it regards our orientation to the intelligible and the true. It is moral inasmuch as it regards our orientation to the good. It is religious inasmuch as it regards our orientation to God. The three dimensions are distinct, so that conversion can occur in one dimension without occurring in the other two, or in two dimensions without occurring in the other one. At the same time, the three dimensions are solidary. Conversion in one leads to conversion in the other dimensions, and relapse from one prepares for relapse from the others. . . . The authentic Christian strives for the fullness of intellectual, moral and religious conversion. Without intellectual conversion he [or she] tends to misapprehend not only the world mediated by meaning, but also the word God has spoken within that world. Without moral conversion he [or she] tends to pursue not what truly is good, but what only apparently is good. Without religious conversion he [or she] is radically desolate: in the world without hope and without God (Eph. 2:12).[19]

Christian educators today must contend with the fullness of conversion and transformation to ensure the present and future vitality of the Christian church in the Americas and throughout the globe. One area in which transformation is called for is in the theological education of the whole people of God, which is explored in the next chapter.

Theological Education
of the Whole People
# of God

The Reformation celebrated the priesthood and, in some cases, the prophethood of all believers. The Christian church at the end of the twentieth century has begun to celebrate the ministry of all believers or the ministry of the whole people of God. The celebration affirms the fact that every believer has gifts for ministry that must be named and exercised. In Latin America, this celebration has included the equipping of all believers for their ministry in the world, which has required the theological education of the whole people of God. Developments in base ecclesial communities with a scarcity of clergy have fostered the efforts to provide theological education for lay leadership. The laity have had to serve in capacities traditionally reserved for the clergy. This situation has affirmed a pastoral vocation for the whole people of God, in which persons serve in a wide variety of ministries to support the work of the church in local communities.

David Stoll suggests that this development in Latin America represents in part the coming of the Reformation to this part of the globe.[1] I suggest that developments in Latin America comprise a new and distinct reformation, beyond the Protestant Reformation, in terms of the access or availability of theological education to the whole people of God. These developments represent a challenge to the dominant patterns of theological education in the United States and suggest the need for a commitment by churches and theological schools to work cooperatively for the theological education of their adult and youth constituencies, in addition to traditional work with children. This cooperative work must connect the ministries of theological and Christian education in more direct ways than have existed in the past.

A question must be raised regarding the distribution of theological educational resources that would enable laity as well as clergy to be equipped for their diverse ministries. The continuation of traditional educational patterns that exclusively separate clergy and laity can be questioned as potentially perpetuating a system that supports a dysfunctional classism. "Classism" refers to any activity, corporately sustained through power, structures, and norms, which unjustly differentiates people on the basis of their social, economic, and professional class affiliation. This unjust differentiation can result in domination, limited options, alienation, and/or assimilation, along with the ascription of negative characteristics to those of a different class. The traditional patterns of theological education may perpetuate the separate class of laity who do not have full access to study and reflection.

In Latin America, a new reformation has included the rise of theological education by extension, sponsored by a vast host of church-related groups and institutions. The sponsoring bodies for such efforts have embraced diverse theological, political, and ideological commitments. This development has been paralleled by the rise of Bible institutes among various groups, but especially among ethnic and pentecostal communities in the United States. Such changes have meant that educational resources are not limited only to those identified as clergy but are accessible to lay persons actively engaged in ministries traditionally designated as pastoral in character. The pastoral calling has been increasingly acknowledged to be the responsibility of the whole people of God, who need training and education to fulfill their ministries.

It is interesting to note that in North America greater attention is often given to developments outside the United States than to similar developments among ethnic communities and those of a more conservative theological persuasion or lower socioeconomic status in the United States itself. The assumption is often made that developments abroad are more significant than those encountered in one's own back yard.[2] In the case of the United States, that back yard includes people whose contributions have been ignored because of the distorted perspectives of both racism and classism. For example, the recent fervor over base ecclesial communities in Latin America as being new forms of the church has failed to recognize similar developments in the United States, which in some cases have predated the emergence of the Latin American forms. However, it appears that ethnic storefront churches in the United States that manifested such forms were not viewed as valid or of consequence because of their social and economic standing. The significant ministries of these communities have been ignored and devalued in part because of the challenge they pose for structures and relationships in the United States, some of which have not been critically examined. The great interest in developments abroad should be complemented by a similar interest in domestic forms, including those that impact upon the role of both the clergy and laity.

The Role of the Clergy

With the increased interest in the ministry of the laity, clergy have had to contend with a renewed understanding of their own role. If the ministry is owned by the whole people of God, what are the unique callings and responsibilities of the clergy? If all Christians have a pastoral calling to care for others, what is the role of the pastor? In response to such questions, clergy have sought to discern the appropriate use of their gifts and authority in relation to an emerging partnership with the laity, a partnership that requires of clergy the reaffirmation of their teaching role and office.

Gabriel Fackre makes the helpful distinction between the ministries of identity that are particular to the clergy and the ministries of vitality that are particular to the laity. These particular ministries do not exclude a common and mutual ministry of both laity and clergy but serve to denote the clergy's primary task of sharing the church's traditions and collective memories as members gather for worship and nurture. By comparison, the laity's primary task is to express the Christian faith in times of being gathered and scattered.[3] This distinction does not suggest that laity lack identity or that clergy lack vitality but that in their corporate and mutual ministry some division of responsibility operates in relation to primary tasks. For laypersons to effectively fulfill their ministries of vitality, the clergy must be faithful in their calling to teach the traditions and the ways in which those traditions need to be transformed to address new challenges. Without this teaching, a foundation is not laid for the formation of Christian identity. Christian identity builds upon the past to understand the present and plan for the future. The distinctions Fackre suggests have not always been applicable to Latin America, where clergy have not always been available to serve the needs of the people. In this situation, laypersons have fulfilled pastoral responsibilities.

With a potential shift in the clergy's understanding of their role, new responsibilities emerge for the clergy in seeking to undergird the ministry of the laity. One of these responsibilities is the need to equip laypersons for their diverse ministries in the world. But clergy may not be prepared to equip laity for unfamiliar ministries. In this case, the clergy must seek to equip and supervise lay leaders who are familiar with such ministries and who themselves can teach and equip others. This seems to be the intent of Paul's mention in Eph. 4:11–12 that the gifts of pastors and teachers, among others given by Christ, is to equip the saints for the work of the ministry. Paul's instructions to Timothy in 2 Tim. 2:2 also suggests that church leaders should entrust the gospel and its teachings to faithful people, who in turn will be able to teach others.

Kennon L. Callahan, the senior consultant at the National Institute for Church Planning and Consultation in Dallas, Texas, argues in *Effective Church Leadership* that the day of the professional minister is over and the day of the missionary pastor has come.[4] Callahan maintains that the professional minister is set over the laity as a professional but that the missionary pastor is one who is in mutual partnership with laity as God's missionaries in the world. The fulfillment of God's mission becomes the central focus rather than the maintenance of the church with its various programs and activities.[5] This new model requires that theological education does not exclusively support the separation of clergy and laity but rather supports the common task of being in partnership with God's mission, which can be defined in terms of the five-task model proposed in chapter 3. This requires of pastors an active teaching role and presence in the local church.

The Pastor as Teacher

In relation to the teaching role of the clergy, an increasing emphasis has emerged in the literature. In 1989, Earl Shelp and Ronald Sunderland edited *The Pastor as Teacher,* a collection of the essays presented as the Parker memorial lectures in theology and ministry at the Institute of Religion in Houston, Texas, in the spring of 1987.[6] In 1989, Robert Browning edited a major work entitled *The Pastor as Religious Educator,*[7] in which an ecumenical group of pastors and religious educators explored ways in which pastors could be more effective in their crucial religious-education role. In 1990, Richard Osmer's work, *A Teachable Spirit: Recovering the Teaching Office in the Church,* was published.[8] Osmer wrote about the need to recover the Reformation heritage of the pastor as teacher through a detailed exploration of the models of Martin Luther and John Calvin. He proposed that seminaries, representative bodies, theologians, and church leaders embrace their calling to participate in a renewed teaching office that impacts upon congregations. A fourth notable work was written by two professors, who significantly are not religious educators; one is a professor of theology and the other a professor of preaching and New Testament. In 1991, Clark Williamson and Ronald Allen coauthored *The Teaching Minister.*[9] Williamson and Allen argued convincingly that the central task of ministry for pastors is teaching the Christian faith and that the need is for theological education of adults in the local church, led by the pastor. By extension, this need is also presented to those institutions that train pastors—namely theological schools and seminaries. Pastors, in their own professional and academic study and formation, need to see models and receive training for this task of teaching laity. Perspectives vary regarding how this might be done and even whether it is the responsibility of theological educators to undertake this task.

One typical pattern that emerges as pastors assume their teaching responsibilities is to teach laity in the same ways in which they themselves were taught. When this occurs, the clergy fails to recognize the aspects of voluntary participation and the dynamics of adult education that are unique to the congregational setting. A pastor does not have a captive audience, as is the case in a schooling experience, and motivations do not usually include the completion of a degree required for active ministry. Clergy therefore must reconceptualize their role as pastors who teach. Any formal classroom education must be complemented by efforts in nonformal and informal education in the life of the congregation.

It is helpful to note that one characteristic cited in the New Testament as a qualification for church leadership is that one be apt or able to teach (1 Tim. 3:2; 2 Tim. 2:24). The ability to teach is seen as a spiritual gift that is given to the church for the common good and edification of the people of God (Rom. 12:7; 1 Cor. 12:28; Eph. 4:11). The gift of pastoring is thus seen to be intimately connected with the effective teaching of believers and those inquiring about the faith. Without such teaching, the continuation of the Christian community is in jeopardy. Therefore, teaching is not optional but essential to the life and health of the local church. The pastor's modeling and support of teaching serves a gatekeeping function. The pastor's explicit commitment can serve to encourage the community to both own and emphasize Christian and theological education. One recognizes that God is the ultimate teacher in any congregational setting, but the pastor has traditionally been viewed as the parson, as God's person in the midst of the faith community, who shares God's perspective on our personal and corporate life.

One assumption of the above discussion is that the pastor of any particular congregation is an effective teacher in actuality or potentiality. This may not be warranted and would then require the identification, training, and support of lay teachers, both within and outside of the congregation, to serve the needs for instruction in the faith. For those pastors who do feel competent to teach as well as for those who do not, this suggests the need for continuing education in the area of teaching. Such continuing education assumes that certain skills for teaching can be taught, while recognizing the distinct gift of teaching which all pastors may not possess. Regardless of their gifts, pastors are called to teach by virtue of their office and are called upon at least to be open to additional gifts from God's Spirit to address the current needs of ministry. As a basic minimum, pastors need to gain some insights to foster and support the teaching ministries of others in their congregations. Not to fulfill this responsibility is to limit the possibilities for present and future generations.

Commitments in Latin America

In Latin America, I was able to visit theological-education programs that were residential and extension, formal and informal, and that served people and communities with educational backgrounds ranging from elementary through higher education. In response to the needs of the churches and the nature of the broad task of the church's mission, a vast host of alternatives have been explored and attempted with varying success. But behind all of these efforts lies the unequivocal commitment to provide equal access to the resources of theological education for the whole people of God.

Levels of Service

Historically, the exploration of alternatives has been prompted by a number of factors named in Ross Kinsler's description of the first innovative effort that occurred at the Presbyterian Seminary in Guatemala.[10] Faithfulness to the gospel and a responsive stance in relation to the needs of the church have necessitated the development of programs and materials for people at three different levels of service, as described by Orlando Costas.

The first and foundational level is comprised of laity who are ministers in their workplaces, communities, homes, and places of leisure. The primary context or ministry of the laity is *in* the world for the sake of the church. The church as scattered during the week seeks to incarnate the Word through its proclamation in deed, through acts of service and mission to humankind. This service is exercised through manifold callings that serve to bring the presence of Jesus Christ to all the nooks and crannies of life. These diverse callings in the world are expressions of the ministries of vitality that Fackre named.

The second level includes the leaders of local and adjudicatory ecclesial bodies, both professional and lay, who provide the local and regional oversight and orchestration of ministry that is faithful to the whole gospel of proclamation, community formation, service, advocacy, and worship. These leaders are Christ's under-shepherds who most visibly incarnate the calling of pastor-teachers.

The third level is composed of the doctors or professors of the church who have the call to develop current and future leadership, to theologically reflect and propose visions in the orchestration of the various ministries of the universal church, and to be architects for renewal through their research, teaching, and mentoring.[11]

Historically, these three levels have been maintained as separate and discrete levels with limited interaction. But this separation and fragmentation could no longer be sustained for a variety of reasons. One reason is the cost of such an arrangement and the need for more equitable distribution of resources. A second reason involves the serious questioning of hierarchical divisions that have replicated the economic, social, and political arrangements in wider society. A third reason relates to a broadened sense of corporate responsibility associated with the ministry of the whole people of God and the awareness of interdependence and partnership in ministry. For partnership to be fostered, joint educational experiences are needed. The need to mix clergy and laity does not negate the complementary need for people of similar callings to "huddle" for specialized education. The problem has been the persistent huddling to the exclusion of adequate mixing and sharing of the theological wealth.

The promotion and implementation of theological education at all three levels have necessitated several commitments that I will discuss in detail in the conclusion of this chapter. First, a commitment to undermine those aspects of professionalism that tend to divide the Christian church is required. Second, a commitment to multicultural education is needed. Multicultural education suggests a type of education concerned with creating educational environments in which participants from all cultural groups will experience educational equity.[12] "Educational equity" can be defined in terms of access to educational resources, respect of difference, space to be heard, appropriate role models, and shared power to make educational decisions. Third, a commitment is called for in relation to holistic theological education. A willingness to risk and explore new forms is required. In this exploration, Christian educators will need to gain insights from both the equilibrium and conflict paradigms and from what each suggests for education.

Equilibrium and Conflict Paradigms

Thomas La Belle, in his study of nonformal education in Latin America and the Caribbean, identified two paradigms that guide the thought and practice of education. These two paradigms of equilibrium and conflict also provide insights for understanding recent developments in both theological and Christian education and represent different basic orientations to the educational change process. The equilibrium paradigm places the emphasis on functional and systems theories, and the conflict paradigm stresses Marxism and cultural revitalization theories.[13] In his study, La Belle draws upon the work of the international educator Rolland Paulston, whose comparative table of educational and social theories surveys options and helps to identify particulars (see table 1).[14]

Paulston indicates that educational reform theories and practices are rooted in systematic ideological orientations concerning social realities and the social change process. Those programs intending to prepare people to take their place as contributing members of existing structures (including the church) in their community and society rely primarily upon the equilibrium paradigm to guide their efforts. Such programs are generally supportive of the current arrangements that can be perpetuated, with education contributing to stability and the adaptation of people to a web of interdependent structures. In contrast, those programs intending to realize radical or even revolutionary changes in existing structures in their community or society rely primarily upon the conflict paradigm to guide their efforts. Such programs are generally not supportive of the current arrangements—given opposing needs and power in a dysfunctional web of structures that serve some and not others—and advocate the role of education in the emergence of new structures.[15] This was the case with my great grandfather's work in Ecuador as described in the Introduction.

A crucial question confronted by educators is how good or bad one assesses the situation in a community or society to be. Is the current arrangement redeemable, reformable, or a total loss? Can the society, structure, or church change? From whose perspective is this possible or not possible? One must also recognize what La Belle noted further, that some educational efforts embody a combination of equilibrium and conflict paradigms because they must simultaneously adapt to existing structures while seeking to reform them or create other structures.[16] In practice, it was this combinationist perspective that most typified the theological educational programs I encountered in my travels in Latin America, but advocates for both equilibrium and conflict paradigms were apparent and, in too many cases, polarized. It is helpful to explore the specific cases of a few programs noting the points of continuity and change with historical efforts. However, before exploring specific cases, it is helpful to name the variables along which educational programs and changes can be assessed.

In returning to the definition of education as a process of sharing content with people in the context of their community and society, it is possible to propose that the three elements of content, persons, and the context be considered. The additional consideration of structures, which is prominent in distinguishing the equilibrium and conflict paradigms, will be included under the element of context because structures set the boundaries of the educational context. The awareness of structures can also assist in the exploration of spaces within and outside of structures where educational innovation may be possible. Structures, from the perspective of a conflict paradigm, may be viewed as confining and limiting, but

Table 1: Theories of Social and Educational Change / "Reform"

Social Change		Illustrative Linked Assumptions Concerning Education-Change Potentials and Processes			
Paradigms	Theories	Preconditions for Educational Change	Rationales for Educational Change	Scope and Process of Educational Change	Major Outcomes Sought
Equilibrium	Evolutionary	State of evolutionary readiness	Pressure to move to a higher evolutionary stage	Incremental and adaptive; "natural history" approach	New stage of institutional evolutional adaptation
	Neo-evolutionary	Satisfactory completion of earlier stages	Required to support "national modernization" efforts	"Institution building" using Western models and technical assistance	New "higher" state of education and social differentiation/specialization
	Structural-Functional	Altered functional and structural requisites	Social system need provoking an educational response; exogenous threats	Incremental adjustment of existing institutions, occasionally major	Continued "homeostasis" or "moving" equilibrium, "human capital," and national "development"
	Systems	Technical expertise in "systems management." "Rational decision making" and "needs assessment"	Need for greater efficiency in system's operation and goal achievement, i.e., response to a system "malfunction"	Innovative "problem solving" in existing systems, i.e., "research and development" approach	Improved "efficiency" re costs/benefits; adoption of innovations

Conflict				
Marxian	Elite's awareness of need for change, or shift of power to socialist rulers and educational reformers	Adjustment of correspondence between social relations of production and social relations of schooling	Incremental adjustment following social mutations or radical restructuring with Marxist predominance	Formation of integrated workers, i.e., the new "socialist man"
Neo-Marxian	Increased political power and political awareness of working class	Demands for social justice and social equality	Large-scale national reforms through "democratic" institutions and processes	Eliminate "educational privilege" and "elitism"; create a more equalitarian society
Cultural Revitalization	Rise of a collective effort to revive or create "a new culture." Social tolerance for "deviant" normative movements and their educational programs	Rejection of conventional schooling as forced acculturation. Education needed to support advance toward movement goals	Creation of alternative schools of educational settings. If movement captures polity, radical change in national educational ideology and structure	Inculcate new normative system. Meet movement's recruitment, training, and solidarity needs
Anarchistic Utopian	Creation of supportive settings; growth of critical consciousness; social pluralism	Free man from institutional and social constraints. Enhance creativity need for "life-long learning"	Isolated "freeing up" of existing programs and institutions, or creation of new learning modes and settings, i.e., a "learning society"	Self-renewal and participation, local control of resources and community; elimination of exploitation and alienation

Source: Rolland G. Paulston, "Social and Educational Change: Conceptual Frameworks," *Comparative Education Review* 21 (1977): 372–73. © 1977 by the Comparative and International Education Society. All rights reserved. Reprinted by permission of the publisher, The University of Chicago Press.

they may also provide the necessary form within which freedom can be expressed.[17]

Content

The element of content can be assessed in relation to what themes and points of view are included and excluded in the educational program. Advocates of the equilibrium paradigm may avoid the naming of conflicts and the exploration of alternative structures that may better serve to address the needs of those historically excluded. In relation to content, questions of readiness, exposure, and the log⁁cal ordering of material may be posed for those who plan, implement, and evaluate any particular program. Advocates of the conflict paradigm may avoid the naming of needed areas of continuity in addition to any changes or discontinuities that may be proposed. In relation to content, questions of the transfer of learning to new situations, questions of the place of creativity, and questions of the transformative or provocative ordering of material may be posed for educators.

Advocates of a conflict paradigm generally propose the reconstruction of some aspects of educational life along with social life. Whether this is warranted on the basis of evidence, history, and need becomes an issue for inquiry and investigation. The same challenge is posed for the advocates of an equilibrium paradigm, who support the continuation of the current structures and systems.

In relation to content, there is a need for dialogue and debate on such issues that afford advocates on both sides, and those somewhere in between, mutual respect and rigor in the development and presentation of their cases. The element of content can also consider the nature of the educational encounter as well as the procedures or methods that are incorporated. In this respect, the method or medium itself can embody the content. The extensive inclusion of debate and the regular posing of conflicts and critical questions can promote the viewpoint of a conflict paradigm. Likewise, the regular use of structured input that limits dialogue through one-way communication and problem-solving techniques that work toward a consensus can promote the viewpoint of an equilibrium paradigm.

Persons

The element of persons can be assessed in relation to both who is present and who is absent from the educational encounter. This is suggested by Guillermo Cook's parable shared at the end of chapter 1. One can also consider the relative power and domination of persons who are present and the efforts to be inclusive of a variety of personal and communal perspectives, even when they represent a minority position on particular issues. Advocates of an equilibrium paradigm would tend to favor the voices of those persons readily accepted as authorities in the existing community and/or society because they insure continuity and stability. Conversely, advocates of a conflict paradigm would tend to honor the prophetic voices who propose new possibilities and see emerging possibilities on the horizon.

The assessment of the element of persons would pose the question of the psychological ordering of the educational experiences of participants. Advocates of a conflict paradigm would hope to empower participants as change agents in their communities and societies, to pose questions and be committed to the needed changes. Advocates of an equilibrium paradigm would hope to prepare participants to occupy positions and maintain perspectives that insure the healthy continuation of existing patterns and structures in the community and society. It is possible to see that a combination of both paradigms may be needed to insure the place of both change and continuity for people across the life span.

Context

The element of context can be assessed in relation to the discussion of contextualization in theological education which has implications for Christian education. The 1972 report, *Ministry in Context: The Third Mandate Programme of the Theological Education Fund*, outlined four areas of contextualization and linked each with a question that is useful in this analysis:

> *1. Missiological contextualization:* Is the program seeking to develop a style of training that focuses on the

urgent issues of renewal and reform in the churches and on vital issues of human development and justice in its particular situation?

2. Structural contextualization: Is the program seeking to develop a form and structure appropriate to the specific needs of its culture in its peculiar social, economic, and political situation?

3. Theological contextualization: Is the program seeking to do theology in a way appropriate and authentic to its situation? Does it offer an approach to education that seeks to relate the gospel more directly to urgent issues of ministry and service in the world? Does it move out of its milieu in its expression of the gospel?

4. Pedagogical contextualization: Is the program seeking to develop a type of education that in its approach attempts to understand the educational process as a liberating and creative process? Does it attempt to overcome the besetting dangers of elitism and authoritarianism in both the methods and goals of its program, to release the potential of a servant ministry among participants?[18]

The consideration of these questions in relation to the element of context would initially appear to favor a conflict paradigm, except for the consideration of structural contextualization which presents the ever-present need for form amid a concern for freedom in the actual practice of education. However, the need for appropriate form and structure may imply a change from existing forms and structures, so long as the place of continuity is at least considered. The advocates of a conflict paradigm must consider the costs of change and what will be substituted in place of existing forms and structures. For example, the Sandinista revolution in Nicaragua did bring about a significant change for some of the poor and oppressed in the nation along with an end to the oppression under the Samoza regime, but it also brought the departure of a number of key professional persons needed for national progress. The advocates of an equilibrium paradigm must consider the costs of continuity and stability along with the obvious gains for certain people and groups. For example, the existing structures in Ecuador support the devaluation of indigenous peoples and cultures, which results in their continued disenfranchisement and a loss of their contributions to the wider society, especially in relation to an emerging ecological crisis.

A similar assessment can be made regarding the perpetuation of the "permanent underclass" in the United States, which includes Native Americans, African Americans, Mexican Americans, and Puerto Ricans, as suggested by the seven-year study of the Carnegie Council on Children completed in 1979.[19] The discussion of social change in relation to educational change is significant because it is often the case that existing educational programs serve to support and perpetuate the present social arrangements of a particular society unless they are intentionally designed to provide alternatives.

The exploration of the three elements of content, persons, and context provides the basis for exploring the following cases of theological education programs using the description of equilibrium and conflict paradigms. The programs of El Seminario Bíblico Latinoamericano (SBL), the Latin American Biblical Seminary, will be considered along with a number of other agencies involved in extension work in Costa Rica, some of which make use of the Personalized System of Instruction (PSI). In addition, I will consider the work of ESEPA, the School of Pastoral Studies, which provided an alternative to SBL. My exposure to programs in Nicaragua, namely Seminario Teológico Bautista (the Baptist Theological Seminary) and CIEETS (the Interecclesial Center for the Study of Theology and Society) was limited and does not warrant detailed evaluation.

Latin American Biblical Seminary

The Latin American Biblical Seminary (SBL) in San José, Costa Rica, was established in 1923 as a result of the vision and work of Dr. Kenneth Strachan and his wife, Susan. For many years, it was closely associated with the Latin America Mission as it sought to provide the biblical and theological formation of pastors, lay leaders, and professors for the churches of Latin America. In 1970, the seminary's leadership began a process of increasing the school's autonomy from its North American missionary affiliations. In 1988 and 1989, the school could be described as having a rich diversity of students from throughout Latin America along with a number of North American professors with significant service as missionaries. In 1980, by a vote of approximately 120 to 15, the comparable Protestant Council of Churches in Costa Rica decided not to support the training of students at SBL because of what was seen as the faculty and administration's commitment to liberation theologies and public support of the Sandinista revolution in Costa Rica's northern neighbor, Nicaragua. The loss of support also involved the disaffiliation from the Latin America Mission and its related church body, the Association of Biblical Churches. The political issues of the separation included the need for autonomous institutional and church government on the part of emerging indigenous leadership in relation to missionary organizations with close North American ties. The call for liberation in theology was paralleled with the call for liberation in self government and direction. The polarized sentiments of this historical break continue among the various church constituencies. The younger church leadership of the Association of Biblical Churches established their own denomination or association.

In this context of theological divergence and church division, SBL has sought to educate the current and future leaders of the Latin American churches. Given the costs of residential study, the seminary has established a vast network of extension centers throughout Latin America, where professors from the residential program, PROENRE, regularly travel to conduct intensive courses. The extension work, PRODIADIS, has a much larger student constituency than the residential program. It also publishes theological texts written at the educational level of extension students. These texts provide professors the opportunity to share the fruits of their scholarship with current and future lay and professional church leaders, with the opportunity for periodic interaction with local extension-center leadership and visiting professors from the San

José central seminary. Leaders of the extension centers annually visit San José to discuss their programs and to address common concerns. This time also serves as an occasion for continuing education and communal sharing. The quality of the residential program has been improved as a result of the learning shared at these annual gatherings and professors' travel has also served to maintain contact with a diverse constituency. This is particularly important because in Latin American higher education political issues readily affect the life and commitments of students, faculty, and administration in direct ways. It is not uncommon to have strikes and confrontations on various issues that impact upon the members of institutions of higher education.

In relation to the areas of content, persons, and the context of community/society, the efforts of SBL can assessed. The range of content of the programs in both the residential and extension programs tended to be quite traditional except for the noteworthy addition of liberation themes and perspectives. The methods used for instruction in the vast majority of courses tended to be typical of higher education. A distinctive dynamic operated in relation to the inclusion of a large number of people traditionally excluded from residential programs through the extension centers and the empowerment of extension-center directors who locally supervised programs and instruction. Another important function was to seriously grapple with the context of Latin America and the realities of poverty and suffering in that setting. The seminary had opted to identify its work with the poor and to emphasize the need for social justice as constitutive of the gospel. In doing so, it was alienated from a number of conservative groups in both the church and missionary community in Costa Rica and Latin America in general. The espousal of liberation theologies for many was associated with a radical Marxist stance that was inconsistent with the gospel. This association was, for the most part, not valid; but it led to further polarization from local church constituencies. However, because of this stance, SBL was viewed as one of the few Latin American theological seminaries in which questions of liberation could be explored. One direct consequence of the polarization was the establishment of an alternative seminary supported by the Asso-

ciation of Biblical Churches—a theologically conservative institution, closely aligned with the Latin America Mission, which had
historically supported the development of SBL. This alternative
seminary was named ESEPA, the School of Pastoral Studies.

The case of SBL points up the danger of a radically politicized
stance in theology, a stance of independence or fundamentalism of
either the left or the right ideologically. New theological insights
must be communicated with and integrated into the life of the
church and not just jettisoned from a distance. New ideas must also
emerge from the churches and the life of the people. Along with
change, continuity is needed in the life of a religious community. A
certain distance is needed for the study and reflection fostered in
theological seminaries, but this must be complemented by active
participation and commitments within the life of the church and its
ministries.

ESEPA

ESEPA grew historically as an alternative to the developments at
SBL in order to serve the needs of a more conservative church
constituency. Unlike SBL, the program at ESEPA did not focus
upon the great social issues of the day. The controlling interest was
the preparation of leadership for local churches that, from one
perspective, were isolated from addressing broader issues. A major
gap in the curricular offerings was in the area of Christian personal
and social ethics. Congregational needs were the order of the day,
with little attention to the community beyond except as the field for
evangelistic outreach. The primary focus was on the spiritual needs
of people served by those who would faithfully preach and teach
the Christian faith.

One innovative course at ESEPA studied and evaluated theological education by extension (TEE) programs and models being used
in Latin America. Several criteria were used in analyzing the programs. The first criterion comprised administrative costs, such as
oversight needed, support services for students, and the training of
teachers and tutors. The second included the methodology of the
materials developed and the perspective of those who developed

the materials. A third criterion comprised the ecclesial link and the utility of the material for the particular local church constituency. This third criterion considered the general availability to the particular local church and to those who would be using the material. The fourth criterion included the purpose of the material and its denominational breadth. What was lacking in the educational program was the gaining of a critical perspective on the content and the implicit theological understanding. Questions could be raised about the transferability of the learning to other contexts encountered by students after their formal study. This also applied in the case of SBL, where the church context did not support a radical agenda of liberation primarily understood in political and social terms. The curriculum at ESEPA required more integrative work with a flexibility for contextualization and reflection upon both personal and corporate experience. Placing greater stress than did SBL upon content, the program at ESEPA might be expected to place secondary importance upon the persons and their context in the community and society, which were the primary foci of SBL.

The extension work done at ESEPA involved the faculty's travel to distant centers for intensive courses. This work provided the professors with the opportunity to see other contexts and to interact on another level, given the wide range of academic abilities represented in the extension settings. Along with the demands upon faculty time to serve extension needs, one challenge for this new school was the process of accreditation. The library size and the lack of a plan for faculty development were possible factors preventing accreditation. In addition, the teaching staff of the school represented a large percentage of North American missionaries, even in comparison with the faculty at SBL which more intentionally recruited Latin American professors.

Personalized System of Instruction

The Personalized System of Instruction (PSI), as is suggested by its very name, attempts to provide individualized instruction for students through the use of prescribed programmed texts that allow people to pursue learning at their own pace outside of a classroom context. This approach has been adopted by a number of extension programs that have their offices in Costa Rica. The material used in the extension programs tends to stress the personal mastery of content. This approach, which radically emphasizes the educational element of persons understood as individuals, can be evaluated in terms of what may be forgotten in the programmed design process. This approach may be very efficient and cost-effective, but one must consider the long-term consequences of its use.

PSI limits the learning that is possible from peers—which, for those learners who learn best from social interaction and dialogue, poses a major drawback. On the other hand, it supports those learners who are more self-directed and capable of independent study and reflection. PSI also limits the impact that the teachers' modeling can provide through the actual classroom or social interaction that is possible in both formal and informal settings that stress group interaction. The majority of programmed texts and workbooks did not provide adequate space for reflection in terms of student written response. They also did not provide for cooperative problem-solving and adequate problem-posing exercises that tend to transfer learnings more readily to what people tend to encounter in real life and ministries. In addition, PSI provided very few opportunities for creative expression because of its primary reliance upon a fill-in-the-blank, paper-and-pencil approach, which required a good deal of regurgitation of the material in prescribed texts.

PSI is appropriate for those elements of instruction that require training—that is, dealing with predictable and replicable situations. However, if the essence of education involves addressing the unpredictable situation, then a narrow focus on training does not best equip persons who must grapple with the changing contours of contexts and the varied applications of content in new and perplexing situations. The unpredictable quality of life may also imply the discovery of new truth and the capacity to perceive it.

With the primary interest in sharing content with individuals, PSI limits the possibility of context specific inquiry except as the application of the shared content. As an alternative, this analysis suggests at some point in the educational process the need for context-specific inquiry with opportunity to reflect on both personal and corporate experience in relation to the content shared. This is best done in a face-to-face encounter with peers and by a teacher who serves as a more experienced observer with wisdom to share. The presence of peers assumes that they too have wisdom to share and questions or problems to pose that individuals need to encounter.

A Comparison

The analysis of SBL, ESEPA, and PSI serves to illustrate the constant challenge in education of balancing the three essential elements of the educational trinity: context, content, and persons. SBL has opted to directly address the context of Latin America with the presence of the poor and the persistent call for liberation and justice. But in addressing the political, economic, and social context, some church members within their immediate context have judged the seminaries to have limited their commitments to a narrow radical constituency and thereby to have become unresponsive to the larger ecclesial and theological context. My judgment differs from this perception, but the polarization has persisted and may require a generation of new leadership to work for reconciliation.

In the case of ESEPA, the institutional commitment has been to maintain a faithful content more readily acceptable to a more conservative ecclesial constituency, which was disaffected with the commitment at SBL to liberation theologies, and a more critical stance regarding North American alliances. This commitment to content has limited the ability to address the relation of the content to the wider social context as evidenced in the curriculum gap in the area of Christian ethics, personal and social. The commitment has also limited the adequate development of younger local leadership to serve as bearers of the content, namely Latin American people who currently and in the future can themselves serve as professors.

In the case of PSI as adopted by extension programs, the limited focus on individual persons can prevent adequate wrestling with the wider communal and societal contexts in which those persons must live and minister. People need critical skills in understanding and responding to this wider reality, which can best be developed through cooperative and interactive educational experiences that are not extensively possible with this approach. In addition, PSI may also limit the extent to which the content itself can be liberating as persons in dialogue with others discover new truth through posed questions and problems that are not outlined in a programmed text.

This comparison does not suggest that the models and practices in North America are any better balanced in relation to the educational trinity. On the contrary, in Latin America, a willingness exists to explore alternatives and attempt new programs that more faithfully seek to theologically educate the whole people of God for the challenges of ministry. The high investment in schooling and formal education in the United States has limited much of the pioneering spirit and openness to new forms that exists in Latin America, from which we can learn. One noteworthy exception has been the efforts of the New York Theological Seminary to develop alternative programs to address the needs of an ethnically diverse urban population.[20]

Retrospect and Prospect

The exploration of alternative forms of theological education beyond current North Atlantic models emerged as a result of various factors in Latin America. These factors included economics, significant church growth, limited educational resources, and grass-roots movements that sought to equip people for diverse ministries no longer provided by professionally trained clergy. The heavy investment required for residential programs was not a possibility. In North America, the exploration of alternative and new forms of theological education on a massive scale will necessitate the passage of time or economic crises. Frequently, change in higher education occurs in the encounter with perceived or actual crises in the life of the church, society, or ecclesial institutions such as theological schools or seminaries. The possibilities of extension models, from the author's perspective, hold the greatest potential in terms of the theological education of the whole people of God—if the North American church embraces fully the implications of the ministry of the whole people of God. Reliance upon the functioning of pastors as teachers in what amounts to a trickle-down theory has not been effective in the vast majority of local church settings. In general, members of the clergy have not been particularly effective in teaching the Christian faith to laity or in equipping the lay teachers in congregations. A broader systemic change is needed— one that follows the history of the popularization of education, where the education of the public first of all implies the theological education of the Christian public best represented by the population of adults and youth in local churches. In the United States, much can be learned from the Bible institutes that serve primarily Pentecostal constituencies.

The other area where alternative forms have and must continue to be explored is in the education of rapidly growing minority church constituencies in the United States. Residential programs have not been readily available to or supportive of the educational needs of ethnic-minority communities, except where there is a genuine commitment to multicultural theological education with the investment of the necessary personnel and material resources for such an educational experience.

The question is not to support either residential *or* alternative forms, such as extension programs in theological education, but residential *and* alternative programs to educate the whole people of God. The challenge is to link the theological education of the professional elite with the Christian education of the masses. The bifurcation is dysfunctional in our time with the pressing need to foster the connections between clerical and lay ministries. Seminaries and theological schools must rethink and reconceptualize their strategic-planning processes at points where new ways can be envisioned for making available both the theological wisdom embodied in the community of scholars and the wisdom of church leaders. Such a dialogue and work must be multilingual to foster the use of the language of various constituencies and publics, not limited to the discourse of the academy, as important as that discourse is.

A joke is shared in Latin America to illustrate this need. "What do we call someone who speaks three languages?" Answer: "Trilingual." "What do we call someone who speaks two languages?" Answer: "Bilingual." "What do we call someone who speaks one language?" Answer: "North American." Being monolingual in a number of ways can restrict and parochialize the ministry of Jesus Christ at the beginning of the next millennium. It is difficult to be partners of those with whom we cannot speak and interact. The professionalization of clerical education has developed some language and communication gaps that require the active acquisition of new languages. The process of globalization necessitates an openness to establish new connections that historically were not possible.

The process of globalization brings into juxtaposition theological education and multicultural education. Multicultural education is discussed in detail in chapter 5. In order to participate fully in both Christian and theological education, lay constituencies need space to initially affirm their cultural identity and context. This affirmation must be followed by the development of critical abilities that enable participants to see the possibilities for transformation where current cultural realities do not conform to or complement Christian values or ideals. Thus, both annunciation and denunciation are required, or proclamation and prophetic advocacy in response to the gospel in each cultural setting. Without this opportunity for annunciation and denunciation, persons and communities do not experience educational equity, nor do they contribute effectively to an ongoing dialogue that is essential for transformative Christian education.

How to Connect?

A very practical question is: "How it is possible to connect or link the educated professionals with the people if, in fact, theological education traditionally associated with clergy can be interfaced with the Christian education of laity?" The work of José Francisco Gomez Hinojosa, a professor in the Pontifical University of Mexico, is helpful in answering this question. Hinojosa wrote *Intelec-*

tuales y Pueblo: Un acercamiento a la luz de Antonio Gramsci, in which he explores the work of Gramsci, an Italian communist thinker, for the work of the church in a polarized situation. Hinojosa suggests that Christian intellectuals organically linked with the laity can offer information, direction, liberating teaching, explanation and formulation, systematization and animation in fulfilling God's mission in the world. In turn, the laity can offer the Christian intellectual a historical proclamation and popular culture with its distinct language, folklore, religion, and common sentiment.[21] In other words, the laity provides the connection of historical and cultural reality, or vitality as Fackre suggested, for the ministry of clergy. In turn, the clergy provide the foundation for Christian identity, Fackre's term, which both laity and clergy share in responding to God's mission in the world.

Clergy and Christian intellectuals share the essential content that provide meaning, whereas the laity provide the grounding both in the people and in the community and society. All bring their gifts to the table and share them in transformative education. Education is the process of sharing content with people in the context of their community and society which necessitates an invitation for all to bring their distinct gifts. This suggests that teaching may best be imaged as an artistically prepared table that welcomes all to partake. Historically, laity have been under the table and without adequate access to all that is shared and to all that they themselves can share to enrich the educational offerings. This deprived not only the laity but also the clergy, who have been feasting at the table without a full menu, without the vital connections to the personal and corporate life of the whole people of God that now are required for the real feast to begin.

New Forces

This chapter suggests that glimpses of the real feast can be seen in Latin America, to which the Christian church in North America must attend. To refuse to attend implies a shortsightedness that has too often characterized North American response to the movement of God's Spirit globally. Glimpses are seen in the alternative forms that have emerged. But why have they emerged? They have emerged as a result of four distinct forces.

First, a sense of crisis develops in which traditional forms are viewed as dysfunctional in response to overwhelming needs in the Christian church and wider society. This crisis emerged in Latin America, but glimpses have been encountered in North America in a time of dwindling resources.

Second, an openness exists to what educators describe as the null curriculum, an openness to those elements or values that have been forgotten or ignored. Most particularly, this includes an openness to the values of indigenous culture, to the *campesinos,* to the poor, and to those on the margins of society. Their concerns and perspectives can no longer be silenced and ignored.

Third, a sensitivity emerges to new challenges in response to God's mission in the world. God is alive, active, and on the move, and calling for a faithful response. This third force is captured well by C. S. Lewis's description in the Narnia chronicles of the anticipation and expectation aroused when news spread that Aslan was on the move. God is going about the work of new things along with sustaining that which is worthy of continuation.

A fourth force, closely related to this third sensitivity, is the emergence of a paradigm shift of major significance. It was initially signalled in the concern for "praxis" voiced by liberation theologians but has moved beyond the limitations of just forging an interface or connections between one's vision and practice, between one's faith and life. With a paradigm shift old systems and values are in need of renewal to provide a new vision that is more comprehensive and integrative.

Contours of a New Paradigm

What are the contours of the new paradigm in Christian and theological education? The paradigm embraces multicultural and multicontextual realities. It embraces the whole people of God as active and contributing participants. It consciously seeks to be integrative and holistic of previous theological polarizations that have separated clergy and laity, continuity and liberation, tradition and transformation, conservative and liberal, ecumenical and evangelical, public and private, the church and the world, the sacred and the secular. This paradigm wrestles with the implications of Christ's ministry for all of life while recognizing the contradictions of being *in* the world and not *of* it as a disciple of Jesus. It recognizes the challenge of proclaiming the particularity of Jesus the Christ in a religiously pluralistic world and seeking to affirm God's universal truth whatever its source. The new paradigm accepts the challenge of speaking the truth in love while working for justice, righteousness, and peace in personal and corporate life. Finally, it recognizes the essential working of God's grace while seeking to express faith through a multitude of works and ministries. All this is done to the end that God might be glorified and enjoyed forever.

Conclusion: New Commitments

Theological education of the whole people of God necessitates several commitments in the context of North America. These were named above but are now explored in greater detail. First, a subversion of the culture of professionalism is required where it leads to an inequitable elitism, exclusivism, classism, and a denial of the existence of a unity in the body of Christ. This commitment does not deny the need for professional competence, integrity, and the accountability of leadership. But it does affirm that the goal and focus of professional preparation and functioning should be service to God, the church, and the world. The concept of service in leadership does not lead to the abuse of clerical authority, but it does demand of persons sacrificial giving that recognizes the place of sabbath, recreation, and personal renewal in the stewardship of one's gifts and time. The approach advocated in this work does not deny the necessary place of specialized education for clergy, but it does recommend the need for the mixing of clergy and laity at key points. The educational huddling of groups with specialized needs must be complemented by educational mixing that shares the wealth needed by all.

A second commitment is required in promoting multicultural

education, which will be discussed in depth in chapter 5. This second commitment requires a genuine interest to encounter the other and a willingness to learn in new ways, especially in a culturally diverse world.

A third commitment is the willingness to risk and explore new forms, even in a time of restricted resources. New wineskins are needed for the new wine in the North Atlantic community. With the disestablishment of the mainline denominations and the public demise of certain evangelical and newline churches, new possibilities can emerge. The perceived arrogance of North American churches must be recognized with the rise of the Christian church in Africa, Latin America, and Asia along with the reemergence of the church in Eastern Europe and the former Soviet Union. The development of an orthodox, ecumenical, evangelical, pentecostal, catholic agenda for the church of Jesus Christ universal requires dialogue that affirms unique theological and denominational identities along with a openness to learn from others and a unity that transcends differences.

Ironically, the dominant stance of being *in* the world in the mainline denominations has resulted in an unconscious denial of what it means not to be *of* the world and the submergence of Christian attributes and identity along with the clear proclamation of the gospel. What is required is the identification of where Christians should not be of the world. This is necessary because of the easy accommodation that has occurred with the dominant culture in the United States. For the newline denominations, what is required is the recognition that Christians are indeed *in* the world, with responsibilities to be about God's business in the world. Easy escapism can no longer be the norm. Ironically, the dominant stance of not being *of* the world has resulted in an unconscious baptism of the world's agenda of success and control, garbed in religious terms, along with the submergence of the Christian mission in the world.

If theological education of the whole people of God is to be more than a popular slogan, new efforts must be made to commit to personnel and material resources in the exploration of new forms and programs. Some past efforts have tended to attract primarily professional, middle-class constituencies, without incorporating people from the working class and from ethnic minorities. A stress upon the *whole* people of God assumes that class distinctions must be overcome in order to faithfully incarnate the gospel in educational practice. The sense of wholeness must also be reflected in the multicultural character of education, which is explored in chapter 5.

Multicultural Christian Education and Values in Hispanic Culture

Double Dutch

As a North American Hispanic, I have been named a new-breed Hispanic.[1] My ethnic heritage is Ecuadorian on my father's side, as celebrated in the introduction, and Dutch and German from Pennsylvania in my mother's lineage. Given the fact that people from German lineage in Pennsylvania are called Pennsylvania Dutch, my daughter names this strand of our family heritage from my mother's roots "double Dutch." It is an appropriate description because "double Dutch" is also the name of a game that my active daughter, Rebekah, enjoys. It is played with two jump ropes turned in tandem and rotating in opposite directions, requiring a unique combination of jumping and coordination to successfully balance oneself. Jumping rope in this way is both a risky and exhilarating activity. This image of jumping double Dutch is appropriate for considering the status of minority people in public and religious education in the United States within a dominant white middle-class ethos.

A Hispanic-American person is conscious of being at a point represented by the position of the hyphen in that term, the position of navigating and balancing the convergence of two cultures that rotate in distinct orbits and require careful coordination and balance. In our pluralistic society with various cultures converging, the image of jumping between two ropes provides insights for negotiating the interaction of elements in multicultural education.

Yet this image is particularly helpful for the new-breed Hispanic population, which Virgil Elizondo describes as *mestizaje*, the origination of a new people from two ethnically disparate parent peoples.[2]

Like the rope game of double Dutch, my life represents the tandem play of two cultures, because I grew up in close association with my father's extended family and cultural roots due to a distancing and disassociation from my mother's family. Yet these extended family ties were immersed in the world of a dominant white local community and culture. Elizondo vividly describes my status and that of others in relation to the experience of people with mixed blood, not unlike the status of being a Galilean in first-century Palestine. Like Galileans, new-breed or new-generation Hispanics are looked down on both by Latin Americans for their cultural impurity and by whites for their ethnic ties. New-breed Hispanics, especially of the third and subsequent generations, are Hispanic in their approach to life, but their first and dominant language is either English or "Spanglish," a mixture of English and Spanish. In most cases, they are not at home in white society and they struggle with the status of being modern-day Galileans.[3] Galilee at its best was a crossroads of cultures and peoples with an openness to each other, not unlike some small communities and associations in my home city, New York. But Galilee at its worst resulted in the exclusion and division of those who were different, not unlike the experience of a vast majority of minority-group members in the United States and some cultural groups in New York City. This experience of exclusion was heightened for me through my marriage to a woman who is of pure Puerto Rican descent. I feel Puerto Rican as an adopted member of my wife's extended family and as a result of six years of ministry in a predominantly Puerto Rican church in East Harlem, New York. Being Puerto Rican and being Hispanic in that context require nurture through a constant effort to reappropriate one's cultural heritage within a dominant culture that has generally sought to squelch it and assign it to an inferior status.

For those of new-breed status who are second-, third-, and subsequent-generation Hispanics in the United States, the distinct challenge is to recover those aspects of Hispanic language and culture that were decimated through decades of discriminatory practices, components of which are ever present in individual and corporate life. This recovery must occur while actively participating in a wider society that devalues this very renewal of Hispanic culture, as evidenced by, for one example, the increased opposition to bilingual education. Such recovery is subject to numerous factors that must be addressed. One factor is the potential danger of further ghettoization, where the maintenance of an ethnic enclave results in alienation from the wider society and an inability to impact upon that society in constructive ways. A second factor is the unwarranted perception by those in the wider society that the affirmation of one's ethnic identity inherently represents an immature longing for one's home group with the attending feelings of security and connection. A third factor is the complex of shifts in a multicultural global existence which necessitate interaction and dialogue on a daily basis across ethnic and cultural divisions. Additional factors can be cited, but the challenge remains to broaden our understanding for addressing such realities. One source of understanding is embodied in the promise of Galilee as Elizondo has prophetically suggested.

The Promise of Galilee

The promise of Galilee at its best can be discerned through exploring some of its history. Galilee, literally denoting a ring or circle, referred to a region comprised of Gentiles and foreigners, of people from various nations. It was a region that was constantly experiencing infiltration and migration. At various times in its history, Galilee was controlled by Babylon, Persia, Macedonia, Egypt, Syria, and Assyria. In the first century, Galilee with a population of approximately 350,000 persons had a large slave element and about 100,000 Jews, who were largely Hellenized. The primary language at this time was Greek Koine, although Jews spoke Aramaic. Thus the Galilean Jews represented a bilingual community. Galilean Jews were lax in the matter of personal attendance at the Temple in Jerusalem, in part for the obvious reason of distance; and this attitude was symbolic of the modified orthodoxy of Jews in Galilee of the Gentiles. It is significant that much of the teaching of Jesus, directed primarily to those living in this context, was not acceptable to the orthodox interpreters of Judea, for he gained a reputation for unusual and controversial interpretation. Jesus manifested a freshness and independence of mind as to the meaning and application of the law, consonant with the religious spirit of Galilee. This region was occupied by a mixed population and had a reputation for racial variety and mixture in and around its borders.[4]

It was in this very setting of Galilee that God chose to be incarnated in the person of Jesus of Nazareth. Yet it is the very nature of this multicultural context that is so often ignored in considering Christian education today. Nevertheless, promise is realized for educators who take heed to the nature of Galilee, which is inclusive of ethnic and cultural diversity. The existence of this region assumes that some form of boundaries were set to define this space and/or the persons occupying it. By focusing on the question of boundaries, which is ever present in human interactions, the Christian educator can explore dimensions of ethnicity and religious faith, particularized in this case from the perspective of the Christian faith. Anya Peterson Royce points out that the maintenance of ethnic identity involves the use of symbolic boundaries from within a group to distinguish it from other groups. Groups maintaining such boundaries celebrate their differences among peoples as distinctive traits and affirm the place of beauty in their culture and ethnic heritage. But at the same time, other boundaries are imposed by external groups upon an ethnic group, reinforcing distinctions. These distinctions too readily become a source of trouble for ethnic groups, fostering ethnic stereotyping, discrimination, and racism. These secondary boundaries isolate differences among peoples as deficits as compared with the positive characteristics maintained by the ethnic groups themselves. Thus there often exist double boundaries—or two ropes—with which ethnic groups must contend.[5]

Ethnic groups that have developed boundaries to define themselves, often in response to a hostile context, can find that additional boundaries have been set to divide them from others. The struggle then becomes how to maintain one's identity and integrity as a member of a minority group and yet fully participate in the larger society, both across defining boundaries and dividing boundaries imposed by that larger society. Those dividing boundaries perpetuate oppression and injustice with a host of complicating factors for ethnic minorities. The struggle becomes how to play double Dutch in being both Hispanic and North American and wanting to play in a way that affirms the significance and integrity of both identities. This conflict is not unique to North American Hispanics, because similar issues can be posed for those who seek to be African and American, Asian and American, or even Christian and North American. Yet the current historical context of the United States and the corresponding emphases upon global and multicultural education provides a unique setting in which to consider the emergence of a new people, new-breed North Americans Hispanics who have experienced the joys and pains of emergence. This emergence offers the opportunity for dialogue and interaction across various cultures in addressing the need for Christian education that seeks to be multicultural. Both the historical and sociological studies of general and religious education have revealed various models of education that have functionally emerged and have been perpetuated in education. Each of these models of education, formulated in relation to ethnic and cultural differences, have primarily patterned themselves after the larger communal contexts of which they are a part.

Context of the United States

The larger context of the United States must be understood in terms of socioeconomic conditions and historical developments. In contrast with Latin America, the United States has historically sustained a larger middle class, which has blurred the distinctions between the oppressed and the oppressors very apparent to the south in the Americas. In recent global economic shifts, the disparities have become more evident in the United States with a widening gap between the rich and the poor. One can also note the popular usage of the term "permanent underclass" to describe a growing segment of the population. The dominant ideology of the United States has also supported the concept of a political democracy while downplaying the realities of economic inequities and the existence of a functional caste system that relegates some citizens to an inferior social and economic status within a market and consumer economy. The additional dynamic is the presence of racial, cultural, and gender distinctions that also correlate with socioeconomic status distinctions. One must also acknowledge the access to education and economic opportunity accorded to limited numbers of persons functionally viewed as members of the lower class or caste, which provides for upward mobility. But for the vast majority of lower-class people, this does not become a reality.

Historically, education in the United States can be analyzed in terms of three major historical periods, as outlined by Lawrence A. Cremin.[6] These are the colonial, national, and metropolitan periods, and each represents a distinct pattern of societal forces and educational ideals that interacted across various institutions seeking to educate an increasingly expanding and diverse population. The five major distinctives that Cremin named in describing the educational history of the United States include the following:

1. A multiplicity of institutions have educated people including the home, community, church or synagogue, economy, school, various social agencies, and the media. The impact of these institutions has varied with individuals and groups, and some people are self-educated.

2. At different times, society has placed its emphases in different institutions with varying success.

3. A concerted effort has been made in the schools to balance the ideals of liberty, equality, and fraternity, which is better understood today as a commitment to the wider community or commonweal.

4. A persistent effort has been undertaken to popularize education, to make it more readily available to all people.

5. The historical perspective reveals that efforts have

been both oppressive and/or liberating, depending upon the persons or groups involved.[7]

It is within this larger context that the various models of education can be considered in the effort to provide educational access to those viewed as culturally and racially different. The ideals of liberty, equality, and fraternity must be evaluated in terms of popularizing education for all cultural groups in the United States.

Models of Education

The various models of ethnic or cultural education are manifest more at the level of the hidden or null curriculum than at that of the explicit curriculum. The explicit curriculum is comprised of the stated and planned events that are intended to be taught and therefore made public. The hidden curriculum includes the sociological and psychological dimensions of education that are largely caught rather than intentionally taught. The null curriculum is that which is not taught or caught but which affects the kinds of options people are able to consider, the alternatives they examine, and the perspectives from which they can view a situation or problem.[8] An investigation of the explicit written curriculum of Christian education, as helpfully undertaken by Charles R. Foster, reveals a progression of models that increasingly favors multiethnic and multicultural pluralism.[9] On the basis of this history of the actual written materials used in Christian education, one could conclude that significant progress is being made in the area of addressing ethnocentrism. But if a researcher explores the actual experiences of minority people and considers what areas of ethnic studies are being forgotten in terms of the null curriculum, a very distinct impression is gained. Whereas the explicit curriculum may explicitly affirm a multicultural education, the hidden and null curricula may operate effectively to undermine that emphasis. This is an-all-too-common experience for ethnic groups who experience the wide gap between what Cremin has termed the "stated intentions" of the explicit curriculum and the "revealed preferences" of the hidden and null curricula.[10] Such is an inevitable consequence of life within a society that does not consistently address the existence of institutional ethnocentrism in its educational efforts.

The works of both Ricardo L. García in general education and of Charles Foster in the history of church education suggest the following four models that currently operate despite a national commitment in the United States to integration and the elimination of some of the effects of racism.[11]

1. White Conformity Model

This model maintains that some people are inferior and marginal because of their cultural, racial, and/or ethnic origin. Such a model perpetuates racial and social exclusion, either intentionally or unintentionally, and devalues the heritage, identity, and experience of people who do not belong to favored ethnic groups. Whereas the vast majority of educational efforts in the United States do not intentionally emphasize conformity at the explicit or stated level, the hidden and null curricula reveal contradictory evidence.

A few examples from personal experience will suffice to illustrate the presence of this model which operates functionally for minority people. My family and I lived in a small-town, New England community with so small a percentage of minority-group members and so parochial an ethos that it essentially functioned from an white-conformity model. The educational experience for our son in the local middle school was typified by the comment of its principal at our first parents' meeting prior to his entrance. One parent asked the principal why only French, and not Spanish, was being taught in the school's curriculum, the explicit curriculum. The principal's response was that Spanish was only needed to use at a local chain restaurant to order Mexican food. One can imagine the extent to which Hispanic and Latin American heritage gained access in this school at the levels of the hidden and null curricula. The middle-school principal lived across the street from our family.

A similar experience confronted our family in a local church, where our daughter was often neglected in her nursery and Sunday School class and overt preference given to children of white heritage. The differential treatment extended to the point that our daughter was actually once physically struck to deal with her cry-ing. When confronted with our daughter's account, the teacher initially denied the incident. No white children in this class received such treatment. Further examples could be cited to illustrate the subtle and not-so-subtle messages that people of ethnic differ-ences received. We were not welcome in the public- and Christian-education programs in this community.

Richard deLone's work, *Small Futures*, describes the functional caste system in the United States that isolates blacks, American Indians, Mexican Americans, and Puerto Rican Americans.[12] My family and I experienced the realities of caste in terms of the hidden and null curricula of the public- and Christian-education offerings in this community sufficiently to signal the presence of an white-conformity model.

2. Melting Pot Model

Historically, this model characterized the educational rationale in the United States prior to the 1960s. As García indicates, the melting-pot model began to show signs of collapse in the 1960s when Nathan Glazer and Daniel Moynihan published the book *Beyond the Melting Pot*. By 1975, the melting-pot model had become intellectually outmoded but not functionally inoperative.[13] A melting-pot or ethnic-synthesis model maintains that all cultures melt down to a common denominator, which in the case of the United States has been white-dominant and English speaking.

The melting pot functions very selectively and can be illustrated by the comments of an African-American seminary student who confided in me about the number of well-intentioned peers who told him that they no longer saw him as a black but as a Christian brother. The place of *koinonia* or community is to be affirmed, but not to the point of failing to recognize who people are ethnically diverse as created by God. Ian Malcolm, an Australian religious educator, has appropriately identified the drive to cultural or ethnic uniformity in the melting-pot model as rooted in human pride and arrogance. From his perspective, ethnic diversity reflects an appro-priate relationship between a transcendent God and a finite human-ity.[14]

The melting pot works to eliminate ethnic distinctivness in the effort to develop a unified identity. It does so not to the extremes of the white-conformity model; nevertheless, distinctive traits are merged in a way that inevitably favors the dominant culture. From the perspective of the minority person, this model might best be compared with a nuclear-reactor meltdown in terms of the destruction of that which is to be preserved in an ethnic heritage. Whereas the white-conformity model seeks to deny and/or obliterate ethnic traits that are not white, the melting-pot model serves to seriously diminish these distinctive traits in relation to the perceived higher good of unity. Whereas the white-conformity model stresses uniformity, the melting pot allows for a unity that, at least at the ideational level, seeks a muted and distorted diversity. These two models place a higher value on unity than on diversity. But this unity is realized at a great cost to people of ethnic backgrounds not viewed as the favored majority or incorporated in the societal norm. The hidden curriculum of a major portion of the educational settings and programs in the United States affirms the values of this melting-pot model.

One may not expect the revolutionary social changes initiated in the 1960s civil-rights movement and resulting legislation to make significant inroads in the value system and ethos of U.S. educational institutions within such a short time. Some progress has been realized at the level of the explicit curriculum, but addressing the hidden and null curricula is a task of long-term magnitude. Work and struggle must continue in this area, but realistic expectations must also be maintained. The recent rise of racial incidents on university (and I might add seminary) campuses are a reminder of the continued efforts that must be extended to realize a more equitable education for minority people in the United States.

3. Cultural-Pluralism Model

This third model stresses the inclusion of racial and ethnic minorities into the life of the nation, community, school, or church. It seeks to have a representative ethnicity as a means by which to pattern global or national realities. At various points in the actual practice of this model, white superiority emerges; but the effort is made to mute overt paternalism.[15] Various ethnic heritages are recognized, but the implicit expectation is that, with maturity, one's ethnic heritage will no longer be emphasized. The message is that people have a right to maintain their ethnic identities, but no one must be carried away with this emphasis in the interest of genuine dialogue and affirmation of a unity that transcends the existent diversity.

This third model is a welcome alternative to the first two, yet it still expects minority people to deny or submerge their heritage rather than celebrate its value as it is offered as a gift to enrich other peoples. This model seeks a unity that essentially displaces one's ethnic identity rather than coexisting in the midst of one's heritage. The choice is posed between either maintaining one's ethnic identity throughout one's life or diminishing its importance in the interest of engagement with the larger cultural plurality. Such terms are not applied equitably to all ethnic groups in the United States because the heritage of some groups is essentially maintained in the existing plurality to a much greater extent. Such a situation parallels that described in George Orwell's *Animal Farm*, where the position of some is "more equal" than that of others. The lack of emphasis upon some ethnic heritages is tantamount to their obliteration in a societal context steeped in racial and cultural domination. For example, if Armenian Americans do not emphasize their cultural heritage, then it will no longer be a gift to this nation or the world because of the genocide experience by this group.

Plurality is encouraged in this model of cultural pluralism but only within the bounds defined by the dominant culture and circumvented by the press for an ill-conceived maturity and unity. A vastly diminished particularity of ethnicity is promoted, which for the North American Hispanics represents a contradiction in terms and commitments. Educationally this model operates to welcome the participation and contributions of representative ethnic groups without addressing the long-term implications of the inclusion and nurture of their ethnicity. Ethnic diversity in this perspective becomes a long-term detriment in favor of a universal agenda that is too narrowly defined. For a person to project a point of maturity in which one no longer celebrates one's heritage and identity is to deny one's person as created by God, even within the purview of the new creation of Jesus Christ.

4. Multicultural Model

As García defines this model, it suggests a type of education committed to creating educational environments in which students from all cultural groups will experience educational equity. Equity is assessed in terms of access to educational resources, respect of difference, space to be heard, the presence of appropriate ethnic role models, and shared power and authority. Multiethnic education is a specific form of multicultural education. It includes not only study of ethnic cultures and experiences but also making institutional changes within the school setting so that students from diverse ethnic groups have equitable educational opportunities.[16] This type of educational format assumes that ethnicity is a salient and continuing part of national and personal life. In this emphasis, a multiethnic or multicultural model moves beyond the model of cultural pluralism. This is the case because those who support multicultural education value the continuing significance of ethnicity throughout the maturing process. Ethnic diversity is maintained and not diminished in the interest of realizing a narrowly defined unity.

A multicultural model suggests two educational movements, the maintenance of both being essential for a proper rhythm and balance. The initial movement is that of emphasizing one's ethnic identity and definition. The complementary movement is that of seeking a common ground for community, for life in a global city grappling with the realities of ethnic and cultural plurality. This second movement involves a quest for universality, for unity, but not at the expense of diversity. The model of cultural pluralism diminishes the first movement in favor of emphasizing the second. This second movement in the multicultural model does not deny one's identity but embodies that identity in dialogue with others from distinct ethnic backgrounds. By its very nature it includes exploring ethnic heritages other than one's own and learning to appreciate them. This dialogue assumes that one has had the luxury and space for grounding one's ethnic identity. Such luxury and space have not been afforded to everyone in the United States, and securing and maintaining that space is crucial in the context of a continuing racially divisive environment. Ethnocentrism is perpetuated on the institutional and personal levels of North American society, even with the explicit advocacy of a multicultural model.

This description of two complementary movements in multicultural education suggests the imagery of double Dutch. A careful coordination of both movements are needed in order to maintain the proper balance of both diversity and unity. The other three models described have in one way or another sacrificed diversity in the interest of unity, with a resulting loss of ethnic distinctivness that provides an essential ground for identity. This unity has been maintained at an unacceptable sacrifice to minority people in the United States. This fourth model is a welcome alternative, with its complementary emphases upon diversity and unity.

With the description of a multicultural model, there remains the question of the basis for unity amidst the vast diversity of ethnic and cultural groups encountered in our world. The Christian claim is that unity is found in Jesus Christ, the Galilean. The resurrected and exalted Christ at Pentecost gifted his followers with the Holy Spirit. The experience of Pentecost points to a multiplicity of ethnic groups and tongues as the first sign of the Spirit's action in bringing healing to a divided world. Pentecost represents the reversal of the divisions of Babel with persons from diverse ethnic and linguistic communities finding unity amidst their diversity as each person heard the gospel in his or her own tongue. The Spirit, on that birthday of the Christian church, pointed to a new source of human understanding and unity, a source embodying people from every race, culture, and language. That source is the Lord Jesus Christ.[17] Personal and communal ethnic identities are not nullified or forgotten with Christian maturity but are transcended in Jesus Christ. This transcendence does not entail denying the gift of ethnicity but sharing that gift with others while receiving the gifts of their heritages as described in a multicultural model. This is Galilee at its best, present at Jerusalem. Thus the question posed for Christians today is not only "What does Athens have to do with Jerusalem?" but also "What does Galilee have to do with Jerusalem?"

Therefore, one can see that a multicultural model of education is to be sought. Double Dutch can be played by incorporating both movements of multicultural education that affirm one's identity and one's participation in the larger world. Double Dutch is played at risk, but that risk is worth taking if one is to be faithful in the task of educating in a pluralistic world. An image of double Dutch, distinct from the rope game and more in tune with the dominant North American culture, is that of sharing equally the costs of an outing among companions. It is a multicultural model that assumes each contributing ethnic group can equally share their heritage and gain from that of others in a climate of mutual respect. To do otherwise is to deny the full implications of the gospel of Jesus Christ and to refuse to address the ethnocentrism resident in each of our lives. What values or distinctive traits can North American Hispanics share as they come to the table with other Christians? What particulars can be affirmed from Latin American and Caribbean sources that make the playing of double Dutch all the more interesting in the United States?

Values in Hispanic Culture

Various scholars have identified the cultural traits and values that are distinctive to North American Hispanics.[18] It is helpful to explore these values in relation to the five tasks of the Christian church named in chapter 3, namely proclamation, community, service, advocacy, and worship, which together make up a holistic vision for the new life in Jesus Christ. In relation to each of the values, it is also possible to name potential weaknesses if a value is stressed out of proportion and relationship to other essential values. The strengths of each value are apparent in their description as alternatives to dominant values in U.S. culture. The naming of weaknesses serves to counter the tendency toward idolatry in celebrating one's cultural heritage which leads to ethnocentrism.

Proclamation as Passion

In relation to proclamation, Hispanic culture values the place of the living or passionate word that is declared and received by all in the community. It is not sufficient just to hear the word, but to embrace it with one's total being becomes essential. In terms of a head, heart, and hand response to what God has done and is doing in the world, Hispanics have particularly valued the heart or soul because from it issues life itself. A passionate response and commitment to the call of Christ is expected from all who would seek to be disciples. Just as Don Quijote, as portrayed by Miguel de Cervantes, passionately pursues life, so Christian believers are called upon to love and follow after God with all of their hearts. This passion is to be balanced with the call to see reality through the ever-present character of Sancho Panza, Don Quijote's constant companion. But the passion is never to be lost in addressing reality. Idealism and realism are partners in the response to the proclamation of the gospel.[19] The stress upon passion and a heart response to the gospel can be a weakness if no attention is given to the place of the head and hand responses as well. Zeal without knowledge and zeal that does not issue in action, just as faith without thought and works, can distort the Christian faith.

Community as *Familia*

In relation to community, Hispanic culture places a high value on the central importance of personal relationships, and in particular the family and community. The family is understood in an inclusive way. The extended family includes in-laws, distant cousins, children, older adults, intimate neighbors, and single people who share a common bond of connection. *Compadres* or *padrinos*, co-parents or godparents by choice, who are related to the family by spirit if not by blood relationships, are also included. This valuing of family extends to the community or *pueblo*, vitally and intimately linking people living in one locale. The *pueblo* is a reality and a symbol of "togetherness, community, and a way of life—integrating language, family, custom, traditions, and other spiritual and cultural traits."[20] The search for community has been persistent in the United States not only in the larger society but in the Christian church itself. Here is a potential gift that Hispanics can offer to the wider multicultural society. A potential weakness in this cultural value is the difficulty of moving beyond the negative aspects of one's family or community of origin with the close bonds of inter-dependence that can foster dependence and squelch independence where it may be needed. The strong ties of family can limit in certain circumstances the emergence of personal identity.

Service as Spirited Work

In terms of the task of service, Hispanic culture has valued passion that is expressed in persistent and spirited work. Some of the hardest-working folks in the United States are Hispanics, whose labor is not rewarded in proportion to their efforts as evidenced by their socioeconomic conditions.[21] Also because of the valuing of personal relationships, Hispanic workers who are valued and supported as full participants in their working community tend to demonstrate a greater sense of loyalty through their service. The potential danger is that this quality of their service makes Hispanics more susceptible to abuse and more reluctant to voice their oppression except when it is extreme and has significantly violated their persons. The struggle for political identity thus becomes a major challenge.

Advocacy as *Mañana*

In relation to advocacy, Hispanic culture has valued the concept of *mañana*. This concept recognizes and accepts the limitations of time and space but embodies an additional dimension named by Justo González in his work, *Mañana: Christian Theology from a Hispanic Perspective. Mañana* embodies "the radical questioning of today."[22] This radical questioning is captured for me in an expression my father often used. Raising his voice in protest, he would say, *"Basta! Basta ya!"* By this he meant, "Enough! Now that is enough!" The voice of advocacy protests those conditions and forces that must be confronted, because enough is enough and changes are demanded. Thus *mañana* holds a promise of a different tomorrow because someone cares enough to confront that which needs to be changed in relation to what God intends for life and makes available through the power of the Holy Spirit.[23] Thus voices of protests and denunciation are raised on behalf of justice, righteousness, and peace because these are the values of God's reign that affect today's realities and deserve our attention. The potential weakness in this value may come in the reluctance to plan carefully in one's passionate advocacy without counting the costs. This can lead to a tendency to be impulsive in relation to a change strategy requiring long-term commitments and efforts.

Worship as *Fiesta*

Finally, in relation to the task of worship, Hispanic culture has valued the place of *fiesta*. *Fiesta* preserves the central place of celebration in life because life itself is a gift that is worth celebrating. This value restores the place of joy that too readily is forgotten in the life of the Christian community and limited to rigidly prescribed occasions. The spirit of *fiesta* embodies a willingness to celebrate at all occasions, even in the midst of suffering. Life continues, and even in death the spirit and life of the deceased continues through the living memory of the family, friends, and community, who are now heirs of the departed's contributions. The motion picture, "The *Milagro* Bean Field War," captured this sense of *fiesta* and portrayed the repeated presence of the deceased elder farmer who periodically reappeared to provide perspective on current happenings in the community. No potential weaknesses of this value can be named because of the urgent need to restore the joy of our salvation and, in the light of our intended end in life and after life, to glorify and enjoy God forever.

However, in a more immediate sense of destiny, Christians are called upon to consider the future in the light of the past and present. Chapter 6 explores possibilities for the future journey together in the Christian church in North America by addressing the challenge of renewing Christian education. That renewal can celebrate the contributions of all ethnic groups as they contribute to a common future.

Possibilities for the Future Journey Together

What possibilities can be suggested for the future of Christian education in the Americas in the light of current developments? Richard R. Osmer, along with others, suggests the need for a recovery of the teaching office in the life of the Christian church in North America.[1] This recovery is essential if Christian education is to remain vital and effective in sharing the Christian faith with current and future generations. The important task of equipping the rising generations for living out the gospel while balancing continuity and change demands the best creative energies and cooperation of various persons committed to the task. In a pluralistic and secular age, sharing the fundamentals of the faith provides the necessary foundation for Christian identity along with an openness to the transformation with which God seeks to grace the church as it confronts new challenges in the world.

Return from Exile: Ezra and Nehemiah

One portion of Scripture that provides a transformative perspective on the task of recovery or renewal of Christian education is represented by the books of Ezra and Nehemiah, which originally comprised one book in the Hebrew Scriptures. Christians have a rich legacy in the Hebrew Scriptures for understanding the task of rebuilding life in the faith community. Ezra and Nehehemiah described the work of rebuilding a nation and rebuilding the lives of those who had returned from exile in Babylon.

The use of biblical literature from the post-exilic period suggests that the exile rather than the exodus may serve as an appropriate motif for the challenges of Christian education in North America. By contrast, in Latin America, the motifs of exodus and liberation have served as key themes for theological reflection. The use of the exile and the return from exile emphasizes the place of rebuilding, renewal, and restoration in the life of the faith community. Given the fact that the United States, following the genocide of American Indians, has developed as a nation of immigrants, exile may historically be more appropriate. Some of the immigrants, like my Ecuadorian ancestors, were exiles from their lands of origin. Some were voluntary and involuntary exiles, but others in the Southwest saw their lands annexed by the United States in its historical expansion. All of these factors suggest that exile may be a more fitting parallel for those currently residing in the United States. In addition, some North American Hispanics feel that they are exiles in a land that was settled by their ancestors before English colonization but is now dominated by a culture that does not affirm Hispanic values. With occupation and foreign domination, a sense emerges of being an exile in one's own land. This situation parallels the experience of the Jews of the Diaspora, who were given an agenda for survival in their exile (Jer. 29:1, 5-9) and an agenda for survival subsequent to it in the books of Ezra and Nehemiah. Unique challenges were posed for the Jews in returning to the land of their ancestors that was under foreign control. As John Yoder suggested in 1973, the complement to the exodus is a "saving message of the resident minority," who speak from their experience of exile.[2] Those on the margins can often offer a liberating perspective for a society by addressing what has been too readily forgotten or ignored by the majority culture. This was the perspective Jesus assumed as a Galilean crucified outside the gate of Jerusalem.[3]

The book of Ezra describes the return of some of the Jewish exiles and the restoration of community life and worship in Jerusalem while it was still under foreign domination. Emperor Cyrus of Persia had commanded this return to rebuild the temple. Ezra helped the people reorganize their religious life and social life in order to safeguard the spiritual, cultural, and social heritage of

Israel. In a similar fashion, the Christian spiritual heritage must also be safeguarded given the ever-present danger of extinction across the generations. The cultural heritage of many marginalized groups must also be preserved.

The book of Nehemiah is notable in its representation of Nehemiah as a lay and political leader who frequently called upon God through prayer for very specific help in times of social need. Chapter 8 of Nehemiah presents a vivid description of the restoration of education that made a difference in the life of the community:

When the seventh month came—the people of Israel being settled in their towns—all the people gathered together into the square before the Water Gate. They told the scribe Ezra to bring the book of the law of Moses, which the Lord had given to Israel. Accordingly, the priest Ezra brought the law before the assembly, both men and women and all who could hear with understanding. This was on the first day of the seventh month. He read from it facing the square before the Water Gate from early morning until midday, in the presence of the men and women and those who could understand; and the ears of all the people were attentive to the book of the law. The scribe Ezra stood on a wooden platform that had been made for the purpose; and beside stood Mattithiah, Shema, Anaiah, Uriah, Hilkiah, and Maaseiah on his right; and Pedaiah, Mishael, Malchijah, Hashum, Hashbaddanah, Zechariah, and Meshullam on his left hand. And Ezra opened the book in the sight of all the people, for he was standing above all the people; and when he opened it, all the people stood up. Then Ezra blessed the Lord, the great God, and all the people answered, "Amen, Amen," lifting up their hands. Then they bowed their heads and worshipped the Lord with their faces to the ground. Also Jeshua, Bani, Sherebiah, Jamin, Akkub, Shabbethai, Hodiah, Maaseiah, Kelita, Azariah, Jozabad, Hanan, Pelaiah, the Levites helped the people to understand the law, while the people remained in their places. So they read from the book, from the law of God, with interpretation. They gave the sense, so that the people understood the reading.

And Nehemiah, who was the governor, and Ezra the priest and scribe, and the Levites who taught the people said to all the people, "This day is holy to the Lord your God; do not mourn or weep." For all the people wept when they heard the words of the law. Then he said to them, "Go your way, eat the fat and drink sweet wine and send portions of them to those for whom nothing is prepared, for this day is holy to our Lord; and do not be grieved, for the joy of the Lord is your strength." So the Levites stilled all the people, saying, "Be quiet, for this day is holy; do not be grieved." And all the people went their way to eat and drink and to send portions and to make great rejoicing, because they had understood the words that were declared to them.

On the second day the heads of ancestral houses of all the people, with the priests and Levites, came together to the scribe Ezra in order to study the words of the law. And they found it written in the law, which the lord had commanded by Moses, that the people of Israel should live in booths during the festival of the seventh month, and that they should publish and proclaim in all their towns and in Jerusalem as follows, "Go out to the hills and bring branches of olive, wild olive, myrtle, palm, and other leafy trees to make booths, as it is written." So the people went out and brought them, and made booths for themselves, each on the roofs of their houses, and in their courts and in the courts of the house of God, and in the square at the Water Gate and in the square at the Gate of Ephraim. And all the assembly of those who had returned from the captivity made booths and lived in them; for from the days of Jeshua son of Nun to that day the people of Israel had not done so. And there was very great rejoicing. And day by day, from the first day to the last day, he read from the book of the law of God. They kept the festival seven days; and on the eighth day there was a solemn assembly, according to the ordinance.

This description of education indicates a head, heart, and hand response of persons to God. Such a response is outlined respectively in verses 1–8 as cognitive understanding is stressed, in verses 9–12 as affective sentiments are addressed, and in verses 13–18 as intentions and actions are described. A holistic response of persons is fostered and expected in the rebuilding effort. In addition, one observes the close linking between worship and education, between the preaching of Ezra with the first mention of a pulpit in the Scriptures, and the teaching of the Levites to provide a sense of what was shared.

It is interesting to note the complementary naming of preaching and teaching in the descriptions of the early church throughout the book of Acts (Acts 4:2; 5:42; 15:35; 20:20; 28:31). In both the exile and in the return from exile, the synagogue arose as a new educational agency that effectively linked together the ministries of worship and education in the life of the faith community. For this connection to be effective in education, the cooperation of a number of key persons was and continues to be fundamental. The relationships among these persons can be described as a partnership with God and others in education.

A Partnership with God and Others

A question to raise in analyzing the Neh. 8 text is "Who were involved in educational renewal?" Four distinct persons or groups can be named. First, God must be recognized as the teacher par excellence. God was at work instructing and restoring the life of the covenant community. God had called Ezra, Nehemiah, the Levites, and a host of people back to the task of rebuilding the wall, the city, and the temple. God called them back to the rebuilding of their personal and corporate lives with education as central to that task.

The centrality of education for the life of a faith community is confirmed by a study completed in 1990 by the Search Institute. One report of this study was Benson and Elkin's *Effective Christian Education: A National Study of Protestant Congregations.* The study surveyed 11,122 people in 561 congregations. The three-and-a-half-year study found that effective Christian education is the most powerful single influence congregations have in helping people grow in faith maturity. This first factor had twice the impact of the other five factors, which are listed below.

1. Members perceive that their congregation encourages questions, challenges thinking, and expects learning.

2. The congregation successfully recruits members to volunteer to help people in need.

3. Members perceive that their Sunday worship is of high quality.

4. Members see their congregation as warm and friendly, having a sense of hospitality.

5. Members personally experience other members' care and concern.

The factor of greatest impact was effective Christian education, which meant that the congregation had a formal Christian-education program including Sunday school classes, Bible studies, adult forums, family events, music and drama programs, and new-member classes.[4] But it is significant to note that education is implied in the other five factors named in the study.

What is the role of the different members of the partnership for effective Christian education?

God as Teacher

The work of God as teacher is noted by the writer of Job, who posed the following question, "See, God is exalted in power; who is a teacher like God?" (Job 36:22) The God of the Hebrew Scriptures is still about the task of teaching humankind. The work of the Trinity, but especially God the Holy Spirit, is indispensable for effective Christian education. The Spirit guides Christians into all truth and glorifies Jesus Christ in the process (John 16:13, 14). God must first be recognized as the first teacher, lest human teachers usurp the place reserved for God in the ministries of Christian education. Human teachers must leave room and expect that God will work in the lives of students, both within and outside of the classroom. Teachers must be reminded of the place of prayer and conscious reliance upon the Holy Spirit in the actual practice of teaching. The ever-present danger is that of idolatry and an intellectual reductionism that fails to embrace the spiritual and supernatural dynamics of teaching that transcend simple formulas and procedures. Such a stance reserves a place for mystery, wonder, and awe in Christian teaching. God's curriculum far exceeds planned and intentional learning activities, to include all of life and a myriad of truths discovered and experiences undertaken. Sensitivity to such a vast curriculum requires an affirmation of the perspective that "ever new light and truth emerges from God's Holy Word." God's Holy Word includes: the Living Word, Jesus Christ; the Written Word of the Scriptures; and the Created Word that embraces all of creation, or what theologians refer to as general revelation. Such a perspective encourages the mind, heart, and soul of persons to go about a daily venture of discovery with the companionship of God and in partnership with others. Who are some of those others as suggested in Neh. 8?

Ezra as Pastor-Teacher

Ezra is the priest and scribe who Jewish tradition designates as "the second Moses" because of his work in reviving Judaism. He stands as a representative of the clergy. As the priest and scribe, Ezra combines the callings of the pastor and scholar. The pastor-teacher, as so named in Eph. 4, has a unique role to play in the life of the faith community. It was Ezra who read the law from daybreak to noon as he was positioned at the high wooden platform, the pulpit. Men, women, and all the children who could understand were gathered to hear Ezra. He had something to share that was worth proclaiming and worth hearing. This description serves to affirm the place of teaching in preaching or proclaiming the Scripture that has import for the whole faith community.

Ezra serves as an example for clergy, an example for pastor-teachers through his devotion or dedication to three essentials tasks. This devotion is described in Ezra 7:1–10, but especially in verse 10. First, Ezra devoted himself to the study of the law of the Lord, to the study of Scripture. Scripture serves as the source of faith and those who serve as leaders must be in touch with the sources for effective ministry.

Second, Ezra devoted himself to the observance of the law, to the observance of what was discerned in God's Word for his life. One of the greatest challenges in an information and knowledge society is that persons are educated beyond their ability to observe or obey what they discern to be God's will. In popular language, the challenge is "to walk the talk." Mere verbalism is insufficient in relating faith to life, a process that calls for concrete commitments and actions consistent with one's faith and that of one's community. Greater devotion to personally and corporately live out one's faith while living in it requires constant diligence and the support of others. Ezra is described as setting his heart to this task of observance. Through such a commitment, the faith is caught as well as explicitly taught.

Third, Ezra was devoted to teaching the law, to teaching God's Word to others as explicitly described in Neh. 8. In recent history, clergy in general have neglected the ministry of teaching. Chapter 4 addressed this concern in the discussion of theological education of the whole people of God, to which clergy must be committed. The Search Institute study revealed that members of the clergy devote an average of 5 percent of their time and energy to teaching in their congregations. A greater level of commitment and participation is needed if Christian-education efforts are to be renewed in the future.

Pastors serve as the gatekeepers for a congregation's life. Even if they are not gifted teachers, pastors must demonstrate a public commitment to educational ministries and must support and equip others in the congregation for their teaching responsibilities. Neh. 8 suggests Ezra's support of the teaching of the Levites through their presence at his side in the public event. The Levites were personally named in the text. This also suggests that the Levites were mutually supportive of Ezra's ministry. Ezra, in this partnership with the Levites and others, was identified as a teacher of the nation.

Daniel O. Aleshire made a provocative observation about this role of teacher in relation to an identity ascribed to Jesus after his resurrection:

> When Mary is shaken from her false assumption about the individual she is addressing in the garden and recognizes the risen Lord, she calls him "Teacher" (John 20:16). He had been friend, healer, preacher, prophet, but when she gasps in the reality of his resurrected presence, she claims him as teacher.[5]

Aleshire points out that at the moment of Jesus' greatest triumph, his resurrection, he is comfortable to be known as teacher.[6] The challenge for pastors in the task of rebuilding Christian education is to demonstrate a similar comfort in being known as teachers and in undergirding the ministry of other teachers in the congregation. As Clark M. Williamson and Ronald J. Allen convincingly argue, the central task of ministry for pastors in North America is teaching the Christian faith. They maintain that the basic need is for theological education of adults in the local church led by the pastor.[7] To neglect this task is to limit the possibilities for present and future generations.

Levites as Teachers

The third party in the proposed partnership for education in Neh. 8 was composed of Levites themselves. The Levites helped the people to understand the law, while the people remained in their places among the assembled congregation. They read from the book, from the law of God, with interpretation. They gave the sense, so that the people understood the reading by Ezra. Without the ministry of the Levites, Ezra's words would have remained unintelligible. It is likely that the Levites were involved in the translation of the words read along with their interpretation.

Walter Brueggemann describes the Levites within Israel as a

priestly group who were entrusted with the office of instruction in the Torah, in God's Word, as they shared a shaping rootage needed by the community.[8] Thus the uniquely educational aspect of this event was the Levites' instruction of the people as they ministered with groups of persons throughout the assembly. They clarified the words of Scripture so that the people could understand. The work of the Levites is paralleled by the ministry of church-school teachers and those who teach through a wide variety of congregational and parachurch ministries including Bible studies, small groups for various ages, and training and discipleship events. All these teachers of the church help the people to see clearly the implications of biblical teachings and encourage the response of persons in ways that are pleasing to God. This response touches on both personal and corporate life. These areas were not divorced in the response of the nation of Israel.

The writer of Ezekiel grasped the importance of the ministry of the Levites when it was observed of them that "They shall teach my people the difference between the holy and the common, and show them how to distinguish between the unclean and the clean. In a controversy they shall act as judges, and they shall decide it according to my judgments." (Ezek. 44:23–24a) Spiritual discernment is as crucial today as it was in Ezra's and Ezekiel's time. Such discernment requires effective ministries of teaching.

In the New Testament, the ministry of the Levitical priests is extended to include the priesthood of all believers as suggested by the teaching of 1 Pet. 2:4–5, 9–10. Christians are a holy and royal priesthood who have been chosen to offer spiritual sacrifices acceptable to God through Jesus Christ. Christians have been chosen to proclaim through their words and actions the mighty acts of God. With Jesus Christ as their eternal high priest, Christians are all members of the priesthood. The Reformation celebrated the priesthood of all believers, and the twentieth century has celebrated the ministry of all believers, which must include the ministries of teaching. The devotion and dedication of the priest Ezra is also required of those who serve as Levites and of those who serve as the contemporary Levitical representatives, Christian teachers of today.

All People as Learners

The fourth party in the partnership, which has been referred to in describing the three entities above, was made up of the people themselves. "The people" comprised the men, the women, and all who could understand, which no doubt included youth and some older children. The people, the hearers, the students, the participants in this worship and teaching event cannot be forgotten. Without the presence of the people, the event would not be noteworthy. The persons, who were not priests or Levites and not God, had responsibilities. The mentioning of "not being God" may seem obvious, but it is significant in terms of a potential danger in some liberation theologies of closely identifying God with the people so that little distinction remains. God's immanence must be complemented with God's transcendence. God's opting for the poor and marginalized does not result in a divinization of the poor. Those sinned against can also manifest sin and be in need of salvation as much as those who oppress. Nevertheless, God's partnership with the people must be celebrated in a time when professionalism and middle-class culture can result in a classism detrimental to the life and teaching of the Christian church.

The responsibilities of the people for education in the faith can be outlined as fourfold. First, the people were to get to know and understand God's Word by attentively listening to its proclamation in both preaching and teaching. Second, they were to embrace God's Word by responding with their hearts to its exposition. Third, they were to obey God's Word by responding with their wills and actions to its exhortation. Fourth, they were to worship God, who was encountered through the proclaimed Word, and to celebrate the restoration God was bringing into their personal and corporate lives. While receiving and responding with their heads, hearts, and hands to the teaching of pastors and teachers, the people were to exercise discernment because they themselves functioned as teachers in their homes, workplaces, and communities. All believers in God are accountable as teachers in a general sense because they are letters in human flesh, read by others (2 Cor. 3:2). Words, actions and attitudes of people impact upon others in variety of ways requiring accountability before God and the wider human community. This accountability includes the quality of life enjoyed in North America at the expense of sisters and brothers to the south.

The Partnership

Being in partnership with God and others in Christian education provides an expansive perspective for the future. It first of all encourages Christians to praise God because God has initiated a partnership with human beings. This partnership is made explicit in the person and work of Jesus Christ and in the continuing ministry of the Holy Spirit. Therefore, the work of Christian education is God's work. God is the ultimate teacher who has called and gifted persons to assist. Those called to assist God in this vital work are assured of God's grace and presence as promised by the resurrected Jesus in his educational commission recorded in Matt. 28:18–20:

> "All authority in heaven and on earth has been given to me. Go therefore and make disciples of all nations, baptizing them in the name of the Father and of the Son and of the Holy Spirit, and teaching them to obey everything that I have commanded you. And remember, I am with you always, to the end of the age."

Being in partnership secondly enables all Christian people to see potentials. Those engaged in teaching are not alone, because others can provide perspective, support, and encouragement. Through the experience of leading teacher-training events in local churches, I have repeatedly found that teachers previously isolated in their teaching have found great support just in realizing that others are confronting similar challenges. With others, persons can see possibilities that they alone cannot see. Jesus was aware of this dynamic in his practice of sending out his disciples in pairs as an extension of his ministry which continues to this day.

Third, being in partnership with God and others empowers Christians to address the problems they are now confronting and will confront in the future. Ministry in and through Christian education incarnates a partnership in suffering and hope in the recognition that one's competence and sufficiency comes from God. In wrestling with problems, people can work for God and with God as well as with others and for others in the Body of Christ. The challenge in addressing problems is to work for the common good in the midst of conflicting interests and needs. Clarity is required regarding God's mission and human cooperation with that mission in the world. Clarity with regard to mission helps to sort through a myriad of needs to discern God's demands as applicable to particular settings. Consensus may not emerge in the process of discernment, and Christians may agree to disagree in certain areas. The oft-quoted wisdom of Rupert Meldinius, the pseudonym of a German Lutheran theologian of the sixteenth century, Peter Meiderlin, is appropriate to name on this point: unity in the essentials, liberty in the incidentals or nonessentials, and in all things charity or love. One perennial problem over the centuries has been the naming of the essentials over which Christians have disagreed, resulting in disunity, contention, and conflict.

Beyond the general mention of both potentials and problems that are implied in affirming the partnership of God and others, specific insights can be identified for the future. These specifics are not intended to be exhaustive but illustrative of new developments on the horizon from my own perspective.

Various Potentials

A specific potential named at the beginning of this chapter but worth reiterating is the faith understanding that God is still our teacher. God the Creator is still active in the world. The other two persons of the Trinity are also active. Jesus is still the Christ, and the Holy Spirit is still a companion and enabler for the believing community. With the discussion of the disestablishment of the mainline churches and the demise of newline churches in the United States, Christians must recognize that God has not been disestablished. Christians in the United States must learn from God's work in other parts of the globe beside Latin America which is the focus of this work. Concerns about the decline of the churches must be directed to an openness and what Richard Osmer named, a "teachable spirit." Christians are called upon to be responsive to God and the continuous work of the Holy Spirit. The attitude implied in this potential is foundational if renewal is to be possible. God's resources have not been depleted. They are eternally renewable, unlike the limited resources of the earth, both material and personal. As a teacher, God is also sovereign, and any future possibilities must be evaluated in terms of the values of God's reign.

A second potential is the current renewed concern with Christian education. The Search Institute study cited above suggested that education should be a top priority for all congregations that want to nurture a vibrant, life-changing faith. Why is there such a new and renewed interest? This interest emerges from an increased awareness that congregations are just one generation away from extinction. Without a renewed interest and commitment, the vitality and continuation of faith communities can be seriously questioned.

A third potential is the emergence of new vision in relation to Christian education and an understanding of the church and its mission, referred to as the theological topics of ecclesiology and missiology. Christian education is being seen increasingly not as a separate and specialized ministry divorced from the entire life of the congregation but as integral and essential for persons across the life span. One expression of this new vision is evident in the rise of various small-group ministries in North America and the rise of base ecclesial communities in Latin America which intentionally seek to support and teach persons the Christian faith close to where those persons live. Another expression is the new appreciation of and experimentation with intergenerational learning that has countered the pervasive age segregation of U.S. society. A third expression of a new vision that is impacting upon the larger society is the rise of communitarianism, which suggests some movement from a "me" to a "we" generation in popular culture. This movement can be fostered in local congregational efforts to form community and to network with wider community concerns as expressions of the gospel.

In congregational life, this new vision is evident in efforts to connect the worship and teaching hours of the church. This is being supported through the use of lectionary-based curricula in some denominations. In addition, local churches are increasingly aware of the fragmentation that exists in modern life. Therefore, a movement exists to return to biblical and theological foundations in seeing the whole ministry of the whole people of God for the world. In such a ministry, laity and clergy are called to work together with God, as suggested in 2 Cor. 6:1 : "In our work together with God, then, we beg you who have received God's grace not to let it be wasted." (TEV) The challenge is for congregations not to waste the potentials that are now presented by God's grace.

A fourth potential currently emerging is the commitment of theological schools and seminaries to the theological education of the whole people of God. In my own workplace, Andover Newton Theological School, a Center for the Ministry of the Laity exists. Historically, its constituency has been primarily limited to white, middle-class, white-collar laity, but changes are emerging for the future to connect with blue-collar working folk and persons from diverse racial and ethnic backgrounds. In addition, a program in its fifth year has brought lay leaders in the field of Christian education to the campus for three intensive weekends of training annually. The name of the program is P.I.E., which refers to "Partners in Education." These programs are not unique and represent a linking of the institutions of theological education with local churches and their denominational bodies in ministries of Christian education.

A fifth potential that can be developed in the upcoming years is the awakening among adult Christians of their need for continuing education in the faith. With the rise of career shifts and retraining required for vocational effectiveness, adults are exposed to the need for teaching that helps them relate the Christian faith to the changing contours of their lives. That teaching may often depart from traditional approaches that were not as sensitive to adult learning styles. Adults were, for many years, a neglected species in Christian-education programs, but that is steadily changing with the commitment to lifelong Christian education.

Program Development Factors

With the naming of these five potentials, the persistent challenge is to develop programs that take advantage of them. In that program development, the findings of the Search Institute study can be of direct assistance. The study identified factors grouped into six categories that contribute to effective Christian education programs.

The first factor is teachers who themselves have mature faith and who know educational theories and methods.[9] This factor has bearing upon the recruitment and selection of teachers. It also implies the need for the equipping, support, and nurture of teachers in the areas of their faith, educational theories, and educational methods. A local church that takes its commitment to teachers seriously will provide for this need through the provision of appropriate training on-site or in cooperation with other local churches or church organizations off-site. It will also make it possible for teachers to regularly attend worship, which implies not always scheduling the educational hour concurrently with worship. This first factor of the teachers' role serves to counter the common strategy for educational change in local church that proposes a curriculum change as the quick fix. Reclaiming the legacy of Hulda Niebuhr would correct this misconception. A former student of hers stated her insight on this matter of curriculum: "What curriculum is used doesn't matter as much as who the teacher is. It is the personal life and faith, the integrity and Christian expression of the teacher which determines ultimately what happens in the classroom."[10] Susanne Johnson also observed, "the most important curriculum is that which is already in teachers."[11] The equipping, support, and recognition of teachers is too often not a congregational priority, with the resulting impact upon the quality of education. The equipping, nurture, and support of teachers does not neglect the need for quality curricular materials for their use.

A second factor category named in the Search Institute study was the role of the pastor in terms of leadership and involvement. A pastor who is committed to education devotes time to Christian education. A pastor who knows educational theory and practice contributes to the development of effective programs and outreach through his or her leadership.[12] As was mentioned above, the pastor often serves as a gatekeeper for Christian-education ministries in the local congregation. The role of lay leaders is essential, but their ministries must be undergirded by pastoral support. The model proposed in chapter 4 implies that the pastor should ideally serve as the theological educator of the congregation. If this is not possible, then others must be empowered for this important responsibility. The theological education of the whole people of God requires an active participation of pastors who work cooperatively with theological schools, denomination staff, and other associations committed to the task of education.

A third factor identified was an educational process that applies faith to current issues, examines life experiences, creates community, recognizes individuality, and encourages independent thinking and questioning.[13] Such a process implies a dynamic interaction and a willingness to dialogue on matters that may engender and celebrate differences as well as points of unity. This process also implies a willingness to grapple with people's questions and doubts. With regard to the question of doubt, Paul de Vries observed that "doubt is the sincere question, but unbelief is the unwillingness to hear the answer."[14] For growth in depth to be possible, a safe space must be created where persons' questions, thoughts, and feelings can be explored. This type of educational process is inherently risky, but well worth the effort to bring faith and life into juxtaposition.

Educational content is named as a fourth general factor. Effective education is associated with educational content that "blends biblical knowledge and insight with significant engagement in the major life issues each age group faces."[15] "Effective adult education emphasizes biblical knowledge, multicultural and global awareness, and moral decision making. Emphases for youth include sexuality, drugs and alcohol, service, and friendship."[16] Attention must be given to educational content along with educational process. The process is to evidence sensitivity to persons and the context of the community and society, and this is also the case for the educational content. This enables the necessary balance in the educational trinity proposed above, where content, persons, and the context of the community and society are all addressed in effective Christian education.

The danger traditionally associated with the thought and practice of education in North America is the overemphasis upon content, in what Paulo Freire referred to as banking education.[17] With more recent developments in North America that have stressed the place of individual, self-directed learning, free from both content and societal constraints, the danger is an overemphasis upon seeing persons as autonomous and separated from the community and society. In Latin America and particularly in the case of educational approaches that have emerged from liberation theologies, the danger is an overemphasis on the reconstruction of the community and society so as to neglect the diversity and continuity of both content and persons within the life of the community and society.

A fifth factor identified in the study was the need for a high percentage of adults to be active in the congregation for there to be effective Christian education.[18] Adults set the tone for congregational life, and their models of participation encourage the involvement of both children and youth. This factor runs counter to the popular notion that if one gets children or youth involved in educational programs, the parents and adults will follow. Clearly the adults must take the lead and sustain their choices and commitments over time if the Christian faith as nurtured in Christian education is to be passed on to succeeding generations. This also suggests the continuing need for children and youth to observe adult models in corporate worship and the need for intergenerational events.[19] Adult participation in the congregation by those who have children and young people in their homes holds the potential of impacting upon family life in positive ways.

The sixth factor from the research summary indicates the need for education programs to have a clear mission and clear learning objectives. The process of determining and evaluating the mission and objectives "builds shared purpose and a sense of a team."[20] Clarity in relation to what a program is attempting and why contributes a great deal to the focus and coordination of efforts. It also contributes to a sense of joy in accomplishing what persons have committed their time and energies to realize. A clear mission and objectives provide a basis for evaluation which may suggest revision of the original mission and objectives. New challenges and avenues for faithfulness to God's mission in the world do emerge and can be identified through evaluation. Frequently, the necessary time is not taken for evaluation, but Christian education efforts can advance through a commitment to evaluate the quality of teaching and learning.

In suggesting potentials for Christian education, one becomes aware of the gap between the ideals identified as potentials and the realities with which persons must contend. In considering the future, those committed to effective Christian education must confront a host of problems. The stance in relation to these problems is not just to be about the task of problem solving. This is the typical North American response. A perspective of problem posing is also needed because the problems initially identified may not address the root causes and the structural or systemic factors that impact upon the thought and practice of Christian education. Paulo Freire named the essential place of problem posing in fostering prophetic and transformative education.[21] A critical perspective is required in appropriating the past, understanding the present, and planning for the future of Christian education. This perspective must be operative in the consideration of problems.

Multiple Problems

To gain perspective on contemporary and emerging problems, it is instructive for Christian educators to return to the example of Nehemiah, who was an effective lay leader used by God in a time of rebuilding and restoration. Nehemiah confronted a number of problems that have some contemporary parallels in Christian education ministries. The educator Lawrence O. Richards has outlined the problems Nehemiah faced and his responses to them.

Nehemiah had the problem of ridicule by his enemies, Sanballat the Horonite, Tobiah the Ammonite official, and Geshem the Arab (Neh. 2:19; 4:1–3). His response was to ask God to vindicate the people while they all ignored the ridicule (2:20; 4:4,5).[22] One of the most difficult challenges in educational ministries, as in all ministry, is dealing with unwarranted and inappropriate criticism. Living in a very critical, and at times cynical, age means that criticism is often used to quickly analyze and dismiss the work of others without recognizing and affirming the positive contributions others make. This requires that those who need to be critical first appropriately affirm the positive aspects in an educational program or effort. It also requires that those being criticized be open to evaluation. If the criticism is confirmed by a number of observers, then it should be heeded and addressed. If the criticism is unwarranted, then it may be dismissed unless further evidence supports the criticism.

A second problem Nehemiah confronted was the plot to attack the builders (4:7–8). Nehemiah's response was to set half the people to work, half to guard with their arms in hand. Along with this preparation, he encouraged Israel to remember God (4:9–23).[23] Various implied plots to attack Christian-education programs and ministries might be conceived, but in local church settings one repeatedly hears of discipline problems in which teachers feel they are under attack. This common problem requires a direct and coordinated effort to understand the reasons for the difficulties with discipline and concrete actions to intervene and provide options for both the teachers and students involved.

A third problem addressed by Nehemiah was that poorer Jews had borrowed from the wealthy. They could not repay their creditors while working on the walls (Neh. 5:1–5). Nehemiah interceded and had the wealthy remit interest and return lands taken from the poor as security (Neh. 5:6–13). He also set an example by supporting himself rather than demanding the governor's allowance that was due him through his service (Neh. 5:14–19).[24] One often encounters budget problems in the support of Christian education, with it being the last to be funded and the first to be cut in hard economic times. A prophetic and confrontational approach may be called for in relation to congregational commitments and the equitable distribution of resources. In relation to the debt service encumbering Latin American nations, the question of debt cancellation can be posed for financial institutions in North America. The question of priorities must be raised in terms of investing in current and future generations. The commitment to the education of children and youth assumes a priority for future generations that must always be held before the church and the wider society.

The fourth major problem Nehemiah confronted was a host of political strategies and maneuvers to undermine and terminate the work. Nehemiah was invited four times to a "counsel" that was a trap set by his enemies (Neh. 6:1–2, 4). He refused to be distracted and kept building the walls (Neh. 6:3). Shemaiah the prophet was hired by his enemies to frighten Nehemiah into hiding in the temple (Neh. 6:10, 12–14). Nehemiah refused to hide from the possible assassins and set an example of courage (Neh. 6:11). Finally, he was threatened with a letter to Artaxerxes saying Nehemiah planned rebellion (Neh. 6:5–7). Nehemiah replied that the enemy had a good imagination, and he kept on with the work (Neh. 6:8–9).[25] Nehemiah sets an example of being decisive in the face of multiple problems. In Christian-education programs, workers and leaders may confront numerous obstacles that seek to divert plans. Nehemiah's example of maintaining both his senses of perspective and humor is noteworthy in his recognition of the good imagination of his enemies. Likewise, Christian educators need to maintain their sense of humor and that of others in gaining perspective on their efforts. In addition, the challenge for Christian educators is to be discerning of the various contextual forces that can both limit and enhance local efforts. Some of these forces represent political decisions and commitments that must be challenged, and others represent the inevitable risks involved in education itself.

Moving beyond the example of Nehemiah, the Search Institute study named the common problems confronted by congregations in the United States. They can be clustered together in five areas. First, time pressures were common in the persistent difficulty of having persons participate. Persons across the life span had busy schedules that limited their availability. In relation to this top-rated problem, the question of priorities, choices, and commitments must be raised. The case in Latin America was that persons set a high priority upon participation in effective Christian-education programs. This also holds for the United States. A second problem was that of recruiting volunteer teachers and leaders. This problem directly relates to the general lack of support, training, and recognition of teachers in congregational life. A third problem is adult and parental disinterest in Christian education that in turn impacts upon the participation of youth and children. A fourth problem was irregular attendance that reduces the continuity and impact of teaching and learning. The fifth major problem was the lack of motivation of teenagers and adults to learn.[26] All these problems require the collective strategizing of clergy and laity committed to Christian education at the local level. No panaceas exist, and the tendency to find quick fixes will limit the spiritual health of current and future generations. Certainly, the naming of potentials above serves to begin the process of developing alternatives and a willingness to learn from what God is doing in such places as Latin America. I am not recommending the replication of Latin American models here but rather a sensitivity to what values and principles undergird effective models elsewhere. In addition, I see two enduring images emerge in looking toward the future of Christian education and discerning possibilities. These images serve as a conclusion to this work.

Two Enduring Images for the Future

The possibility of two enduring images was suggested to me on a trip I took in the summer of 1990 with other theological educators to the U.S./Mexican border. On that trip, we visited a local church in Tucson, Arizona, that has been active in the sanctuary movement. That movement has sought to support refugees from Latin America who have come to the United States. Many of these have fled their homelands for a variety of reasons that include political, economic, social, and religious oppression. Prominently displayed in that local church where the south meets the north in a striking way, is a cross draped with a *sarape*, a Mexican blanket of many colors. The sight is a study in contrasts for a North American who is accustomed to seeing only an unadorned cross in typical Protestant churches. Draped over the extended horizontal arms of the cross was a garment typically worn by Mexican persons for everyday and festive occasions. Two distinct objects carrying cultural and religious meanings were brought into relationship, suggesting a new and provocative combination. This image was not unlike that of double Dutch, with the two ropes turning in tandem; but in this case, the two elements combined were strikingly different.

A similar study in contrasts can be imagined in relation to two enduring images that have graced the life of the Christian church throughout the ages. These images are those associated with two church ordinances or sacraments regularly celebrated in local congregations throughout the Americas and worldwide. These two enduring images serve as a paradigm for the thought and practice of Christian education for the present and future as they have in the past. They are baptism and eucharist.

Baptism is a universal practice in the Christian church, though it is celebrated at different points in the life of Christians within distinct traditions. I personally had the experience of both infant and believer's baptism, reflecting the blending of my father's previous Roman Catholic heritage and my mother's Baptist tradition. So, in a literal sense, I stand in an Anabaptist (meaning baptized again) legacy. Baptism serves as the public act of initiating persons into the community of faith and, in the case of adult baptism, serves as a confirmation of one's conversion and faith in Jesus Christ.[27] Baptism can also be seen as the initial sign of one's lifelong vocation in following Jesus.

The eucharist is called by different names in various traditions. But what is noteworthy for Christian education is that, whereas baptism is generally a single event in the lives of believers, with noted exceptions, communion is a repeated event, suggesting a process of God's continued grace, presence, and nurture in the lives of believers. The repeated nature of Holy Communion or eucharist is celebrated each season, month, week, or even more frequently in some Christian traditions and practices.

What, then, is the connection between these sacraments and Christian education? Baptism serves as a paradigm for those aspects of Christian education that stress the need for change, conversion, and transformation in human life. Such change and conversion is posed in a context where conflict is apparent and persons must make choices and commitments in terms of life and death. In current historical perspective, this is the dominant concern in the context of Latin America and those places in North America where people have been marginalized and severely oppressed. Hence, the emphasis on liberation from the destroyers of life in the people's struggle for survival. Consciousness of this reality is important for North American Christians as they strive to live out the implications of their baptism, which implies a calling to serve the least of our sisters and brothers in Latin America and in North America, all deserving of God's grace and human care.

Holy Communion serves as a paradigm for those aspects of Christian education that stress the need for nurture and the gradual process of growing in the grace and knowledge of the Lord Jesus Christ. These aspects of education tend to emphasize the place of equilibrium and balance to optimize the points of continuity in personal and corporate life. This perspective has tended to characterize the efforts of Christian education in North America and, in those cases where stability has been the norm, in Latin America.

But can anyone imagine a Christian church in which both baptism and eucharist are not celebrated in the life of the faith community? Likewise, the separation of perspectives between the North and the South in the Americas cannot be sustained in the Christian church. The emergence of North American Hispanics suggests the futility of such a stance and the need for a teachable spirit that enables persons across traditional geographical, cultural, economic, and political divisions to care deeply enough to listen and respond together to God's mission in new and creative ways. Much can be learned to enrich the thought and practice of Christian education in North America by seeing what God is doing in Latin America. A southward journey of the mind and spirit offers new insights for followers of Jesus Christ in addressing current and future challenges in Christian education and other areas of ministry. The prayer that accompanies this work is for the willingness of Christians to journey not only south, but east, west, and north in serving the Christ of all nations and in recognizing the cultural barriers Jesus Christ has shattered.

Notes

Introduction

1. Justo L. González points out that: "Nineteen years before the British founded their first colony in the land that Sir Walter Raleigh called Virginia, the Spanish based in Cuba founded a city that exists in Saint Augustine, Florida. And twelve years before the Pilgrims landed on Plymouth Rock, the Spanish founded the city of Santa Fe, New Mexico." See Justo L. Gonzalez, *Mañana: Christian Theology from a Hispanic Perspective* (Nashville: Abingdon, 1990), 31.

2. In the case of Costa Rica, the extensive use of chemicals banned in the United States for agricultural production has resulted in a high incidence of stomach cancer among the Costa Rican population. The tragedy of this situation for me is that Dr. Orlando Costas, the former Academic Dean of Andover Newton Theological School, was the person who encouraged me to visit Costa Rica given his ten-year service there as a missionary. Orlando died in Nov. 1987 at the age of forty-five after a courageous six-month battle with stomach cancer. Dr. Costas was one of the foremost missiologists in the world at the time of his death.

3. For a more detailed description of Alfaro's presidency, see David B. Pazmiño, "General Eloy Alfaro and the Rise of Liberalism in Ecuador 1895–1911," B.A. honors thesis, Wesleyan University, Middletown, Conn., 1993.

4. Jacques M. P. Wilson, *The Development of Education in Ecuador* (Coral Gables, Fla.: University of Miami Press, 1970), 48–49.

Chapter 1

1. See Enrique Dussel, *A History of the Church in Latin America*, trans. Alan Neely (Grand Rapids: Eerdmans, 1981).

2. Guillermo Cook names these destroyers as challenges that the Latin American churches must confront in "Eclesiología y realidad centroamericana: pistas misiologicas," *Vida y Pensamiento* 7 (Enero–Diciembre 1987): 92.

3. See José Miguez Bonino, "Statement by José Miguez Bonino," in *Theology in the Americas*, eds. Sergio Torres and John Eagleson (Maryknoll, N.Y.: Orbis, 1976), 278.

4. Irene W. Foulkes, "Protestant Churches and Social Change in Central America," a work to be published in *Churches and Change in Latin America*, ed. Margaret Crachan (La Jolla: Institute of the Americas, forthcoming), manuscript pages 8–9.

5. Gustavo Gutierrez, *A Theology of Liberation: History, Politics and Salvation*, trans. Sister Caridad Inda and John Eagleson (Maryknoll, N.Y.: Orbis, 1973), 36–37, 176.

6. Guillermo Cook, *The Expectation of the Poor: Latin American Communities in Protestant Perspective* (Maryknoll, N.Y.: Orbis, 1985), 238.

7. See Orlando E. Costas, "Educación Teologica y Misión," in *Nuevas Alternativas de Educación Teologica*, ed. C. René Padilla (Buenos Aires: Nueva Creación, and Grand Rapids: Eerdmans, 1986), 9.

8. See Rosino Gibellini, *The Liberation Theology Debate*, trans. John Bowden (Maryknoll, N.Y.: Orbis, 1987), 20.

9. José Miguez Bonino, *Doing Theology in a Revolutionary Situation* (Philadelphia: Fortress, 1975), 87.

10. Gabriel Fackre, *The Christian Story: A Narrative Interpretation of Basic Christian Doctrine*, rev. ed. (Grand Rapids: Eerdmans, 1984), 23.

11. See Leslie Newbigin, *Foolishness to the Greeks: The Gospel and Western Culture* (Geneva, Switz.: World Council of Churches, and Grand Rapids: Eerdmans, 1986), 58.

12. Abraham J. Heschel, *An Introduction*, vol. 1 of *The Prophets* (New York: Harper Colophon Books, Harper & Row, 1969), 200–201.

13. Ibid., 201.

14. Orlando E. Costas, *Christ Outside the Gate: Mission beyond Christendom* (Maryknoll, N.Y.: Orbis, 1982).

15. Dorothee Soelle, *Suffering* (Philadelphia: Fortress, 1975), 70–73.

16. Robert McAfee Brown, *Theology in a New Key: Responding to Liberation Themes* (Philadelphia: Westminster, 1978), 66.

17. This document has been translated. See "Document: The Medellin Declaration on Liberation Theology," *Latin American Pastoral Studies* 16 (July 1989): 133–58. The journal's editor hopes that this translation will encourage the open dialogue within North American and European evan-

gelicalism concerning the challenge to the church from Latin American theology. I share this hope.

18. Samuel Solivan, "Orthopathos: Interlocutor between Orthodoxy and Praxis," *Andover Newton Review* 1 (Winter 1990): 19–25.

19. Guillermo Cook, *Let My People Live: Faith and Struggle in Latin America* (Grand Rapids: Eerdmans, 1988), xiv–xv.

Chapter 2

1. Robert W. Pazmiño, *Principles and Practices of Christian Education: An Evangelical Perspective* (Grand Rapids: Baker, 1992), 10–11.

2. See the detailed work of Daniel S. Schipani, *Religious Education Encounters Liberation Theology* (Birmingham, Ala.: Religious Education Press, 1988); and Matías Preiswerk, *Educating in the Living Word: A Theoretical Framework for Christian Education,* trans. Robert R. Barr (Maryknoll, N.Y.: Orbis, 1987) for a discussion of the relationship between liberation theologies and religious education.

3. John Elias provides a description of Freire's work in "Paulo Freire: Religious Educator," *Religious Education* 71 (Jan.-Feb. 1976): 40–56.

4. Sara Little, "Theology and Religious Education," in *Foundations for Christian Education in an Era of Change,* ed. Marvin J. Taylor (Nashville: Abingdon, 1976), 31–33.

5. Norma H. Thompson, "Current Issues in Religious Education," *Religious Education* 73 (Nov.-Dec. 1978): 617.

6. Paulo Freire, *Pedagogy of the Oppressed,* trans. Myra Bergman Ramos (New York: Seabury, 1970), 36.

7. See Paulo Freire, "Education, Liberation and the Church," *Risk* 9 (1973): 40–46 for a description of his three views of religion.

8. Paulo Freire, "The Educational Role in the Churches in Latin America," in Latin American Documentation Series of the U.S. Catholic Conference (LADOC) 3 (Dec. 1972): 19.

9. Rubem Alves, *Educaco Telogica para a Liberade* (Sao Paulo, Brazil: Simposio, 1970), 14.

10. F. Ross Kinsler, "Extension: An Alternative Model for Theological Education," in *Learning in Context* (Cromley, Kent, Eng.: Theological Education Fund, 1973), 29.

11. Freire, "Education, Liberation and the Church," 34.

12. George W. Webber, "Innovation in Theological Education: Reflections from the United States," in *Learning in Context* (Bromley, Kent, Eng.: Theological Education Fund, 1973), 96–97.

13. Marie Augusta Neal, *A Socio-Theology of Letting Go: The Role of a First World Church Facing Third World Peoples* (New York: Paulist, 1977), 43–44.

14. Victor Nazario, "Theological Education and the Third World: Searching for Fundamental Issues," in *Learning in Context* (Bromley, Kent, Eng.: Theological Education Fund, 1973), 18–26.

15. Harvie M. Conn, "Contextualization: Where Do We Begin?" in *Evangelicals and Liberation,* ed. Carl E. Armerding (Nutley, N.J.: Presbyterian and Reformed, 1977), 117.

16. *Ministry in Context: The Third Mandate Programme of the Theological Education Fund (1970–1977)* (Bromley, Kent, Eng.: The Theological Education Fund, 1972), 78.

17. William A. Dyrness, *Learning about Theology from the Third World* (Grand Rapids: Zondervan, 1990), 20–21.

18. Paulo Freire, *Cultural Action for Freedom* (Cambridge, Mass.: Harvard Educational Review and Center for the Study of Development and Social Change, 1970), 20.

19. Denis E. Collins, *Paulo Freire: His Life, Works and Thought* (New York: Paulist, 1977), 77–87.

20. Ibid., 4, 16.

21. Freire, *Pedagogy of the Oppressed,* 75–76.

22. Kinsler, 40–41.

23. Robert McAfee Brown, *Theology in a New Key: Responding to Liberation Themes* (Philadelphia: Westminster, 1978), 71.

24. Webber, "Innovation in Theological Education," 98, 99.

25. Freire, "Education, Liberation and the Church," 35–36.

26. Elias, 55.

27. Paulo Freire, *Pedagogy of the Oppressed,* 19.

28. Paulo Freire, *Education for Critical Consciousness* (New York: Seabury, 1973), 19.

29. Elias, 52.

30. Ibid., 55–56.

31. Ibid., 42–46.

32. For a discussion of these criticisms, see Orlando E. Costas, *The Church and Its Mission: A Shattering Critique from the Third World* (Wheaton, Ill.: Tyndale, 1974), 219–64; and Clark H. Pinnock, "Liberation Theology: The Gains and Gaps," *Christianity Today* (16 Jan. 1976): 13–15.

33. Schipani, 188–90.

34. Lawrence A. Cremin makes this distinction in *Public Education* (New York: Basic Books, 1976), 50.
35. Schipani, 190.
36. Freire, "Education, Liberation and the Church," 36.
37. Aharon Sapsezian, "Theology of Liberation—Liberation of Theology: Education Perspectives," *Theological Education* 9 (Summer 1973): 267.
38. Ministry in Context, 46–49.

Chapter 3

1. Portions of this chapter originally appeared in Robert W. Pazmiño, "A Comprehensive Vision for Conversion in Christian Education," *Religious Education* 87 (Winter 1992): 87–101; and Robert W. Pazmiño, *Principles and Practices of Christian Education*, 37–57, which discusses principles of Christian education for the present and future. Used by permission of the publishers. The focus here is on insights gained from my Latin American journey.

2. See David T. Abalos, *Latinos in the United States: The Sacred and the Political* (Notre Dame, Ind.: University of Notre Dame, 1986), 133. Abalos defines transformation as "the conscious breaking of inadequate patterns, the movement through confusion, and the creation of fundamentally new and better patterns that capacitate people to experience themselves, one another, their sacred sources, and problems afresh" (p. 89). It is noteworthy that Abalos names the five faces of capacity in transformation that parallel the five tasks of the church named below. The five faces are a new consciousness (related to proclamation and identity), creativity (related to service), linked power in community (related to faith community), shared justice (related to advocacy), and a new connection to the sacred as the source of capacity (related to worship) (p. 163).

3. For a helpful discussion of transformation and conversion in the New Testament, see Beverly Roberts Gaventa, *From Darkness to Light: Aspects of Conversion in the New Testament* (Philadelphia: Fortress, 1986). Gaventa argues for at least three types of conversion: alternation, pendulumlike conversion, and transformation. She states: "Alternation occurs when change grows out of an individual's past behavior. It is the logical consequence of previous choices. Pendulum conversion involves the rejection of past convictions and affiliations for an affirmed present and future. Transformation applies to conversions in which a new way of

perception forces the radical reinterpretation of the past. Here the past is not rejected but reconstructed as part of a new understanding of God and world" (p. 148). The discussion of conversion in this chapter emphasizes pendulum conversion and transformation more than alternation. For an extensive study of conversion see V. Bailey Gillespie, *The Dynamics of Religious Conversion: Identity and Transformation* (Birmingham, Ala.: Religious Education Press, 1991); and H. Newton Malony and Samuel Southard, eds., *Handbook of Religious Conversion* (Birmingham, Ala.: Religious Education Press, 1992).

4. John Marsh, "Conversion," in *The Interpreter's Dictionary of the Bible*, ed. George A. Buttrick (Nashville: Abingdon, 1962), 678. Also see John M. Mulder, "Conversion," in *Harper's Encyclopedia of Religious Education*, eds. Iris V. Cully and Kendig B. Cully (San Francisco: Harper & Row, 1990), 160–63.

5. John Marsh, "Conversion," 678.

6. C. Ellis Nelson, *How Faith Matures* (Louisville: Westminster/John Knox, 1989), 112.

7. Ibid., 113.

8. Richard Peace, "The Conversion of the Twelve: A Study of the Process of Conversion in the New Testament," Ph.D. diss., University of Natal, South Africa, 1990. Peace discusses conversion in terms of the three movements or phases of insight, turning, and transformation. He argues for a holistic understanding of conversion as a process.

9. As cited in N. H. Beversluis, *Toward a Theology of Education: Occasional Papers from Calvin College*, 1:1 (Feb. 1981), 19.

10. See Hugh T. Kerr and John M. Mulder, eds., *Conversions: The Christian Experience* (Grand Rapids: Eerdmans, 1983), for an account of the experience of various persons in relation to their conversions.

11. Orlando E. Costas, *Liberating News: A Theology of Contextual Evangelization* (Grand Rapids: Eerdmans, 1989), 113. For a full discussion of the call to conversion, see chapter 6 of this work which describes conversion as a series of new challenges, new turnings, and new experiences that are rooted in Christ and expressed in a distinctive quality of life. Bernard Lonergan provides a similar analysis from his perspective in *Method in Theology* (New York: Herder & Herder, 1972), 130–31, where he sees conversion normally as a prolonged process though its explicit acknowledgement may be concentrated in a few momentous judgments and decisions. Rather than a series of developments, Lonergan portrays conversion as a resultant change of course and direction in life to a new and distinct world and a new relationship with history, one's community,

and one's culture. For a discussion of Lonergan's work in relation to religious education, see Thomas H. Groome, "Conversion, Nurture and Educators," *Religious Education* 76 (Sept.-Oct. 1981): 482–96.

12. For further discussion of these points, see Robert W. Pazmiño, *Foundational Issues in Christian Education: An Introduction in Evangelical Perspective* (Grand Rapids: Baker, 1988), 111–13. Ronald T. Habermashas suggested in response to my work that this definition is paralleled in Paul's summative testimony of "The Way" in Acts 24:14–16 in the following three points: information is expressed in Paul's belief in the "law and prophets" (v.14), and especially the resurrection (v.15); formation is present in the shape of Paul's resultant "hope" (v.15) and worship as a life response (v.14); and transformation is suggested in both the vertical and horizontal dimensions of a clear conscience (v.16). Thus these three verses can serve as a summary of the Christian walk of faith. I maintain that transformation is possible in the case of individual persons as well as the community and society, but for lasting historical impact the changes experienced by individuals need to affect the community and society.

13. A helpful introduction to this history is provided by Marianne Sawicki, *The Gospel in History: Portrait of a Teaching Church: The Origins of Christian Education* (New York: Paulist, 1988).

14. For further study regarding the role of the pastor in the educational ministry of the church, see Earl E. Shelp and Ronald H. Sunderland, eds., *The Pastor as Teacher* (New York: Pilgrim, 1989); Robert L. Browning, ed., *The Pastor as Religious Educator* (Birmingham, Ala.: Religious Education Press, 1989); and Clark M. Williamson and Ronald J. Allen, *The Teaching Minister* (Louisville: Westminster/John Knox, 1991).

15. It is interesting to note a parallel between the five tasks named here and the models of the church proposed by Avery Dulles in *Models of the Church*, expanded ed. (Garden City, N.Y.: Doubleday, 1987). The church as herald is related to proclamation, as mystical communion to community, as servant to service, as institution to advocacy, and as sacrament to worship.

16. Bonino, *Doing Theology in a Revolutionary Situation*, 87.

17. For a host of other examples, see the case studies in Alice Frazer Evans, Robert A. Evans, and William Bean Kennedy, *Pedagogies for the Non-Poor* (Maryknoll, N.Y.: Orbis, 1987).

18. Orlando Costas, *Liberating News*, 116.

19. Bernard Lonergan, *Doctrinal Pluralism* (Milwaukee: Marquette University, 1971), 34–35.

Chapter 4

1. See David Stoll, *Is Latin America Turning Protestant?: The Politics of Evangelical Growth* (Berkeley: University of California Press, 1990); and David Stoll, "A Protestant Reformation in Latin America?" *Christian Century* (Jan. 17, 1990): 44–48.

2. This preference for developments abroad is identified as "xenocentrism" in chapter 2.

3. Gabriel Fackre, "Christ's Ministry and Ours," in *The Laity in Ministry: The Whole People for the Whole World*, eds. George Peck and John S. Hoffman (Valley Forge, Pa.: Judson, 1984), 110–15.

4. Kennon L. Callahan, *Effective Church Leadership: Building on the Twelve Keys* (San Francisco: Harper & Row, 1990), 3.

5. Ibid., 13–34.

6. Shelp and Sunderland, eds.

7. Robert L. Browning, ed.

8. Richard R. Osmer, *A Teachable Spirit: Recovering the Teaching Office in the Church* (Louisville: Westminster/John Knox, 1990).

9. Williamson and Allen.

10. F. Ross Kinsler, "Kairós en la Educación Teológica," *Vida y Pensamiento: Nuevos Caminos en la Educación Teológica Latinoamericano* 8 (Diciembre 1988): 16.

11. Orlando E. Costas, "Educación Teológica y Misión," in *Nuevas Alternativas de Educación Teológica*, ed. C. René Padilla (Buenos Aires: Nueva Creación, and Grand Rapids: Eerdmans, 1986), 12–14.

12. See the work of Ricardo L. García, *Teaching in a Pluralistic Society: Concepts, Models, Strategies* (New York: Harper & Row, 1982), 8.

13. Thomas J. La Belle, *Nonformal Education in Latin America and the Caribbean: Stability, Reform or Revolution* (New York: Praeger, 1986), 42–46.

14. See Rolland G. Paulston, *Conflicting Theories of Social and Educational Change* (Pittsburgh: University Center for International Studies, University of Pittsburgh, 1976); and Rolland G. Paulston, "Social and Educational Change," *Comparative Education Review* 21 (1977): 370–95. For a discussion of Paulston's work as related to Christian education, see Robert W. Pazmiño, *Foundational Issues in Christian Education*, 168–72.

15. La Belle, *Nonformal Education*, 42.

16. Ibid.

17. For a discussion of educational structures, see Robert W. Pazmiño,

Principles and Practices of Christian Education, chapter 3, "Educational Structures."
18. *Ministry in Context,* 31.
19. Richard H. deLone, *Small Futures: Children, Inequality, and the Limits of Liberal Reform* (New York: Harcourt Brace Jovanovich, 1979), 153.
20. See Robert W. Pazmiño, *The Seminary in the City: A Study of New York Theological Seminary* (Lanham, Md.: University Press of America, 1988); and George W. Webber, *Led By The Spirit: The Story of New York Theological Seminary* (New York: Pilgrim, 1990).
21. José Francisco Hinojosa, *Intelectuales y Pueblo: Un Acercamiento a la Luz de Antonio Gramsci* (San José, Costa Rica: Editorial Departamento Ecuménico de Investigaciones, 1987), 228–46.

Chapter 5

1. Themes from this chapter were initially explored in my article "Double Dutch: Reflections of an Hispanic North-American on Multicultural Religious Education," *Apuntes* 8 (Summer 1988): 27–37. This article was selected to appear in *Voces: Voices from the Hispanic Church, Selections from the First Ten Years of Apuntes,* ed. Justo L. González (Nashville: Abingdon, 1992), 137–45.
2. Virgil Elizondo, *Galilean Journey: The Mexican-American Promise* (Maryknoll, NY: Orbis, 1983).
3. Orlando Costas, "Evangelizing an Awakening Giant: Hispanics in the U.S.," in *Signs of the Kingdom in the Secular City,* comps. David J. Frenchak and Clinton E. Stockwell, ed. Helen Ujvarosy (Chicago: Covenant, 1988), 57.
4. K. W. Clark, "Galilee," in *Interpreter's Dictionary of the Bible,* ed. George A. Buttrick (Nashville: Abingdon, 1962), 344–47.
5. Anya Peterson Royce, *Ethnic Identity: Strategies of Diversity* (Bloomington: Indiana University, 1982), 18–19.
6. For a detailed discussion of these historical developments, see Lawrence A. Cremin, *American Education: The Colonial Experience 1607–1783* (New York: Harper & Row, 1970); Lawrence A. Cremin, *American Education: The National Experience 1783–1876* (New York: Harper & Row, 1980); and Lawrence A. Cremin, *American Education: The Metropolitan Experience 1876–1980* (New York: Harper & Row, 1988).

7. Lawrence A. Cremin, lecture presented at Teacher's College, Columbia University, New York, 18 Dec. 1978.

8. Elliot Eisner makes these distinctions in *The Educational Imagination: On the Design and Evaluation of School Programs*, 2nd ed. (New York: Macmillan, 1985), 87–108.

9. Charles Foster, "Double Messages: Ethnocentrism in the Education of the Church," *Religious Education*, 82 (Summer 1987), 447–67.

10. Cremin, *Public Education*, 50.

11. See García, 37–57; and Foster.

12. deLone, 153–60.

13. García, 37–45.

14. Ian Malcolm, "The Christian Teacher in the Multicultural Classroom," *Journal of Christian Education*, 74 (July 1982), 48–60.

15. Foster, 457–58.

16. García, 8, 105.

17. Marina Herrera, "The Hispanic Challenge," *Religious Education* 74 (Sept.-Oct. 1979), 458.

18. See Virgil Elizondo, "A Bicultural Approach to Religious Education," *Religious Education* 76 (May-June 1981): 258–70; Herrera, 457–63; Abalos, 159–66; and especially Eldin Villafañe, *The Liberating Spirit: Toward an Hispanic American Pentecostal Social Ethic* (Lanham, Md.: University Press of America, 1992), 3–24.

19. Villafañe vividly describes this paradox in *The Liberating Spirit*, pp. 6–7.

20. Ibid., p. 20.

21. Ibid., pp. 32–36.

22. Justo González, *Mañana: Christian Theology from a Hispanic Perspective* (Nashville: Abingdon, 1990), p. 164.

23. Ibid.

Chapter 6

1. See Osmer, who proposes the contours of the recovery by drawing upon the examples of Martin Luther and John Calvin.

2. John H. Yoder, "Exodus and Exile: The Two Faces of Liberation," *Cross Currents* 23 (Fall 1973): 304–305. Also see George W. Webber, *Today's Church: A Community of Exiles and Pilgrims* (Nashville: Abingdon, 1979).

3. This perspective from the margin is explored in Costas, *Christ Outside the Gate*.

4. For a report of the study, see Peter L. Benson and Carolyn H. Elkin, *Effective Christian Education: A National Study of Protestant Congregations, A Summary on Faith, Loyalty, and Congregational Life* (Minneapolis: Search Institute, 1990). For a brief popular summary of the findings, see Eugene C. Roehlkepartain, "What Makes Faith Mature?" *Christian Century* 107 (May 9, 1990): 496–99.

5. Daniel Aleshire, "Finding Eagles in the Turkeys' Nest: Pastoral Theology and Christian Education," *Review and Expositor* 85 (1988): 704.

6. Ibid., 705.

7. Williamson and Allen, 7, 13–14.

8. Walter Brueggemann, "Teaching as Witness: Forming an Intentional Community," in *The Pastor as Teacher,* eds. Earl E. Shelp and Ronald H. Sunderland (New York: Pilgrim, 1989), 37, 59.

9. Benson and Elkin, 53–64.

10. Rev. Paul Krebil to Elizabeth Caldwell, 13 April 1988, Chicago. For an exposure to Hulda Niebuhr's legacy, see Elizabeth F. Caldwell, "Remembering Hulda Niebuhr," *Religious Education* 86 (Winter 1991): 52–61.

11. Susanne Johnson, *Christian Spiritual Formation in the Church and Classroom* (Nashville: Abingdon, 1989), 140.

12. Benson and Elkin, 53–64.

13. Ibid.

14. Paul de Vries, "The Deadly Sin," *Christianity Today* (May 15, 1987): 22. Also see Habermas, 402–10.

15. Benson and Elkin, 54.

16. Roehlkepartain, 498.

17. Freire, *Pedagogy of the Oppressed,* 59–66.

18. Roehlkepartain, 498.

19. For additional discussion of the place of children in worship, see David Ng and Virginia Thomas, *Children in the Worshipping Community* (Atlanta: John Knox, 1981); and Dennis C. Benson and Stan J. Stewart, *The Ministry of the Child* (Nashville: Abingdon, 1978). For a study of intergenerational educational events, see James W. White, *Intergenerational Religious Education: Models, Theory and Prescription for Interage Life and Learning in the Faith Community* (Birmingham, Ala.: Religious Education Press, 1988).

20. Benson and Elkin, 54.

21. Freire, *Pedagogy of the Oppressed,* 66–74.

22. Lawrence O. Richards, *The Teacher's Commentary* (Wheaton: Victor Books, 1987), 310.

23. Ibid.
24. Ibid.
25. Ibid.
26. Benson and Elkin, 38.
27. For a detailed study of baptism and eucharist, see Robert L. Browning and Roy A. Reed, *The Sacraments in Religious Education and Liturgy* (Birmingham, Ala.: Religious Education Press, 1985).

Bibliography

Abalos, David. *Latinos in the United States: The Sacred and the Political.* Notre Dame: University of Notre Dame Press, 1986.

Aleshire, Daniel. "Finding Eagles in the Turkeys' Nest: Pastoral Theology and Christian Education." *Review and Expositor* 85 (1988): 695–709.

Alves, Rubem. *Educaco Teologica para a Liberade.* Sao Paulo, Brazil: Simposio, 1970.

Benson, Dennis C., and Stan J. Stewart. *The Ministry of the Child.* Nashville: Abingdon, 1978.

Benson, Peter L., and Carolyn H. Elkin. *Effective Christian Education: A National Study of Protestant Congregations, A Summary on Faith, Loyalty, and Congregational Life.* Minneapolis: Search Institute, 1990.

Beversluis, N. H. *Toward a Theology of Education: Occasional Papers from Calvin College* 1 (Feb. 1981): 1–32.

Bonino, José Miguez. *Doing Theology in a Revolutionary Situation.* Philadelphia: Fortress, 1975.

——. "Statement by José Miguez Bonino." In *Theology in the Americas,* edited by Sergio Torres and John Eagleson, 275–79. Maryknoll, N.Y.: Orbis, 1976.

Brown, Robert McAfee. *Theology in a New Key: Responding to Liberation Themes.* Philadelphia: Westminster, 1978.

Browning, Robert L., ed. *The Pastor as Religious Educator.* Birmingham, Ala.: Religious Education Press, 1989.

Browning, Robert L., and Roy A. Reed. *The Sacraments in Religious Education and Liturgy.* Birmingham, Ala.: Religious Education Press, 1985.

Brueggemann, Walter. "Teaching as Witness: Forming an Intentional

Community." In *The Pastor as Teacher,* edited by Earl E. Shelp and Ronald H. Sunderland. New York: Pilgrim, 1989.

Caldwell, Elizabeth F. "Remembering Hulda Niebuhr." *Religious Education* 86 (Winter 1991): 52–61.

Callahan, Kennon L. *Effective Church Leadership: Building on the Twelve Keys.* San Francisco: Harper & Row, 1990.

Clark, K. W. "Galilee." In *Interpreter's Dictionary of the Bible,* edited by George A. Buttrick, 344–47. Nashville: Abingdon, 1962.

Collins, Denis E. *Paulo Freire: His life, Works and Thought.* New York: Paulist, 1977.

Conn, Harvie M. "Contextualization: Where Do We Begin?" In *Evangelicals and Liberation,* edited by Carl E. Armerding, 907–119. Nutley, N.J.: Presbyterian & Reformed, 1977.

Cook, Guillermo. "Eclesiología y Realidad Centroamericana: Pistas Misiologicas." *Vida y Pensamiento* 7 (Enero-Diciembre 1987): 78–100.

————. *The Expectation of the Poor: Latin American Base Ecclesial Communities in Protestant Perspective.* Maryknoll, N.Y.: Orbis, 1985.

————. *Let My People Live: Faith and Struggle in Latin America.* Grand Rapids: Eerdmans, 1988.

Costas, Orlando E. *Christ Outside the Gate: Mission beyond Christendom.* Maryknoll, N.Y.: Orbis, 1982.

————. *The Church and Its Mission: A Shattering Critique from the Third World.* Wheaton, Ill.: Tyndale, 1974.

————. "Educación Teológica y Misión." In *Nuevas Alternativas de Educación Teológica,* edited by C. René Padilla, 9–22. Buenos Aires: Nueva Creación, and Grand Rapids: Eerdmans, 1986.

————. "Evangelizing an Awakening Giant: Hispanics in the U.S." In *Signs of the Kingdom in the Secular City,* compiled by David J. Frenchak and Clinton E. Stockwell, edited by Helen Ujvarosy, 55–64. Chicago: Covenant, 1988.

————. *Liberating News: A Theology of Contextual Evangelization.* Grand Rapids: Eerdmans, 1989.

Cremin, Lawrence A. *American Education: The Colonial Experience 1607–1783.* New York: Harper & Row, 1970.

————. *American Education: The National Experience 1783–1876.* New York: Harper & Row, 1980.

————. *American Education: The Metropolitan Experience 1876–1980.* New York: Harper & Row, 1988.

————. *Public Education.* New York: Basic Books, 1976.

deLone, Richard H. *Small Futures: Children, Inequality, and the Limits of Liberal Reform.* New York: Harcourt Brace Jovanovich, 1979.

de Vries, Paul. "The Deadly Sin." *Christianity Today* 31 (May 15, 1987): 22–24.

"Document: The Medillin Declaration on Liberation Theology." *Latin American Pastoral Studies* 16 (July 1989): 133–58.

Dulles, Avery. *Models of the Church.* Expand. ed. Garden City, N.Y.: Doubleday, 1987.

Dussel, Enrique. *A History of the Church in Latin America,* translated by Alan Neely. Grand Rapids: Eerdmans, 1981.

Dyrness, William A. *Learning About Theology from the Third World.* Grand Rapids: Zondervan, 1990.

Eisner, Elliot W. *The Educational Imagination: On the Design and Evaluation of School Programs.* 2d ed. New York: Macmillan, 1985.

Elias, John. "Paulo Freire: Religious Educator." *Religious Education* 71 (Jan.-Feb. 1976): 40–56.

Elizondo, Virgil. "A Bicultural Approach to Religious Education." *Religious Education* 76 (May-June 1981): 258–70.

————. *Galilean Journey: The Mexican-American Promise.* Maryknoll, N.Y.: Orbis, 1983.

Evans, Alice Frazer, Robert A. Evans, and William Bean Kennedy. *Pedagogies for the Non-Poor.* Maryknoll, N.Y.: Orbis, 1987.

Fackre, Gabriel. *The Christian Story: A Narrative Interpretation of Basic Christian Doctrine.* Rev. ed. Grand Rapids: Eerdmans, 1984.

————. "Christ's Ministry and Ours." In *The Laity in Ministry The Whole People for the Whole World,* edited by George Peck and John S. Hoffman. Valley Forge: Judson, 1984.

Foster, Charles. "Double Messages: Ethnocentrism in the Education of the Church." *Religious Education* 82 (Summer 1987): 447–67.

Foulkes, Irene W. "Protestant Churches and Social Change in Central America." In *Churches and Change in Latin America,* edited by Margaret Crachan. La Jolla: Institute of the Americas, in press.

Freire, Paulo. *Cultural Action for Freedom.* Cambridge, Mass.: Harvard Educational Review and Center for the Study of Development and Social Change, 1970.

————. *Education for Critical Consciousness.* New York: Continuum, 1973.

————. "Education, Liberation and the Church." *Risk* 9 (1973): 34–48.

————. "The Educational Role in the Churches in Latin America." *LADOC* 3 (Dec. 1972): III.14, 1–14.

————. *Pedagogy of the Oppressed*, translated by Myra Bergman Ramos. New York: Seabury, 1970.

García, Ricardo L. *Teaching in a Pluralistic Society: Concepts, Models, Strategies.* New York: Harper & Row, 1982.

Gaventa, Beverly Roberts. *From Darkness to Light: Aspects of Conversion in the New Testament.* Philadelphia: Fortress, 1986.

Gibellini, Rosino. *The Liberation Theology Debate,* translated by John Bowden. Maryknoll, N.Y.: Orbis, 1987.

Gillespie, V. Bailey. *The Dynamics of Religious Conversion: Identity and Transformation.* Birmingham, Ala.: Religious Education Press, 1991.

Glazer, Nathan, and Patrick Moynihan. *Beyond the Melting Pot.* Cambridge, Mass.: Harvard University Press, 1963.

González, Justo L. *Mañana: Christian Theology from a Hispanic Perspective.* Nashville: Abingdon, 1990.

————, ed. *Voces: Voices from the Hispanic Church, Selections from the First Ten Years of Apuntes.* Nashville: Abingdon, 1992.

Groome, Thomas H. "Conversion, Nurture and Educators." *Religious Education* 76 (Sept.-Oct. 1981): 482–96.

Gutierrez, Gustavo. *A Theology of Liberation: History, Politics and Salvation,* translated by Sister Caridad Inda and John Eagleson. Maryknoll, N.Y.: Orbis, 1973.

Habermas, Ronald T. "Doubt Is Not a Four-Letter Word." *Religious Education* 84 (Summer 1989): 402–10.

Herrera, Marina. "The Hispanic Challenge." *Religious Education* 74 (Sept.-Oct. 1979): 457–63.

Heschel, Abraham H. *The Prophets.* Vol. 1, *An Introduction.* New York: Harper & Row, 1969.

Hinojosa, José Francisco. *Intelectuales y Pueblo: Un Acercamiento a la Luz de Antonio Gramsci.* San José, Costa Rica: Editorial Departamento Ecuménico de Investigaciones, 1987.

Johnson, Susanne. *Christian Spiritual Formation in the Church and Classroom.* Nashville: Abingdon, 1989.

Kerr, Hugh T. and John M. Mulder, eds. *Conversions: The Christian Experience.* Grand Rapids: Eerdmans, 1983.

Kinsler, F. Ross. "Extension: An Alternative Model for Theological Education." In *Learning in Context.* 27–49. Bromley, Kent, Eng.: Theological Education Fund, 1973.

————. "Kairós en la Educacíon Teológica." *Vida y Pensamiento* 8 (Dec. 1988): 16–28.

La Belle, Thomas J. *Nonformal Education in Latin America and the Caribbean: Stability, Reform or Revolution.* New York: Praeger, 1986.

Little, Sara. "Theology and Religious Education." In *Foundations for Christian Education in an Era of Change,* edited by Marvin J. Taylor, 30–40. Nashville: Abingdon, 1976.

Lonergan, Bernard. *Doctrinal Pluralism.* Milwaukee: Marquette University Press, 1971.

———. *Method in Theology.* New York: Herder & Herder, 1972.

Malcolm, Ian. "The Christian Teacher in the Multicultural Classroom." *Journal of Christian Education* 74 (July 1982): 48–60.

Malony, H. Newton, and Samuel Southard, eds. *Handbook of Religious Conversion.* Birmingham, Ala.: Religious Education Press, 1992.

Marsh, John. "Conversion." In *The Interpreter's Dictionary of the Bible,* edited by George A. Buttrick. Nashville: Abingdon, 1962.

Ministry in Context: The Third Mandate Programme of the Theological Education Fund (1970–1977). Bromley, Kent, Eng.: Theological Education Fund, 1972.

Mulder, John M. "Conversion." In *Harper's Encyclopedia of Religious Education,* edited by Iris V. Cully and Kendig B. Cully, 160–63. San Francisco: Harper & Row, 1990.

Nazario, Victor. "Theological Education and the Third World: Searching for Fundamental Issues." In *Learning in Context.* 18–26. Bromley, Kent, Eng.: Theological Education Fund, 1973.

Neal, Marie Augusta. *A Socio-Theology of Letting Go: The Role of a First World Church Facing Third World Peoples.* New York: Paulist, 1977.

Nelson, C. Ellis. *How Faith Matures.* Louisville: Westminster/John Knox, 1989.

Newbigin, Leslie. *Foolishness to the Greeks: The Gospel and Western Culture.* Geneva, Switz.: World Council of Churches, and Grand Rapids: Eerdmans, 1986.

Ng, David, and Virginia Thomas. *Children in the Worshipping Community.* Atlanta: John Knox, 1981.

Osmer, Richard R. *A Teachable Spirit: Recovering the Teaching Office in the Church.* Louisville: Westminster/John Knox, 1990.

Paulston, Rolland G. *Conflicting Theories of Social and Educational Change.* Pittsburgh: University of Pittsburgh Press, 1976.

———. "Social and Educational Change: Conceptual Frameworks." *Comparative Education Review* 21 (1977): 370–95.

Pazmiño, David B. "General Eloy Alfaro and the Rise of Liberalism in

Ecuador 1895–1911." B.A. honors thesis, Wesleyan University, Middletown, Conn., 1993.

Pazmiño, Robert W. "A Comprehensive Vision for Conversion in Christian Education." *Religious Education* 87 (Winter 1992): 87–101.

————. "Double Dutch: Reflections of an Hispanic North-American on Multicultural Religious Education." *Apuntes* 8 (Summer 1988): 27–37.

————. *Foundational Issues in Christian Education: An Introduction in Evangelical Perspective.* Grand Rapids: Baker, 1988.

————. *Principles and Practices of Christian Education: An Evangelical Perspective.* Grand Rapids: Baker, 1992.

————. *The Seminary in the City: A Study of New York Theological Seminary.* Lanham, Md.: University Press of America, 1988.

Peace, Richard. "The Conversion of the Twelve: A Study of the Process of Conversion in the New Testament." Ph.D. diss., University of Natal, South Africa, 1990.

Pinnock, Clark H. "Liberation Theology: The Gains and Gaps." *Christianity Today* (Jan. 16, 1976): 13–15.

Preiswerk, Matías. *Educating in the Living Word: A Theoretical Framework for Christian Education,* translated by Robert R. Barr. Maryknoll, N.Y.: Orbis, 1987.

Richards, Lawrence O. *The Teacher's Commentary.* Wheaton, Ill.: Victor Books, 1987.

Roehlkepartain, Eugene C. "What Makes Faith Mature?" *Christian Century* 107 (May 9, 1990): 496–99.

Royce, Anya Peterson. *Ethnic Identity: Strategies of Diversity.* Bloomington: Indiana University Press, 1982.

Sapsezian, Aharon. "Theology of Liberation—Liberation of Theology: Education Perspectives." *Theological Education* 9 (Summer 1973): 254–67.

Sawicki, Marianne. *The Gospel in History: Portrait of a Teaching Church: The Origins of Christian Education.* New York: Paulist, 1988.

Schipani, Daniel S. *Religious Education Encounters Liberation Theology.* Birmingham, Ala.: Religious Education Press, 1988.

Shelp, Earl E., and Ronald H. Sunderland, eds. *The Pastor as Teacher.* New York: Pilgrim, 1989.

Soelle, Dorothee. *Suffering.* Philadelphia: Fortress, 1975.

Solivan, Samuel. "Orthopathos: Interlocutor between Orthodoxy and Praxis." *Andover Newton Review* 1 (Winter 1990): 19–25.

Stoll, David. *Is Latin America Turning Protestant?: The Politics of Evangelical Growth.* Berkeley: University of California Press, 1990.

———. "A Protestant Reformation in Latin America?" *Christian Century* Jan. 17, 1990: 44–48.

Thompson, Norma H. "Current Issues in Religious Education." *Religious Education* 73 (Nov.-Dec. 1978): 611–26.

Villafañe, Eldin. *The Liberating Spirit: Toward an Hispanic American Pentecostal Social Ethic.* Lanham, Md.: University Press of America, 1992.

Webber, George W. "Innovation in Theological Education: Reflections from the United States." In *Learning in Context.* 94–115. Bromley, Kent, Eng.: Theological Education Fund, 1973.

———. *Led by the Spirit: The Story of New York Theological Seminary.* New York: Pilgrim, 1990.

———. *Today's Church: A Community of Exiles and Pilgrims.* Nashville: Abingdon, 1979.

White, James W. *Intergenerational Religious Education: Models, Theory and Prescription for Interage Life and Learning in the Faith Community.* Birmingham, Ala.: Religious Education Press, 1988.

Williamson, Clark M. and Ronald J. Allen. *The Teaching Minister.* Louisville: Westminster/John Knox, 1991.

Yoder, John H. "Exodus and Exile: The Two Faces of Liberation." *Cross Currents* 23 (Fall 1973): 297–309.

Index

Advocacy, 71–73, 121–22
Alfaro, General Eloy, xvii–xxi, 147
Anthropology, 10

Banking education, 32, 44, 140
Baptism, 144–46
Base ecclesial communities, 67, 136
Bonino, José Miguez, 3–4, 11, 65

Celebration, 73, 122
CELEP, xxvi, 9
Central America, xxvi–xxvii
Christian education: definition of, 61; five-task model of, 62–63, 64; new paradigm of, 102–3; potentials, 135–37; problems, 141–44; sacraments in, 144–46; as transformative, 35, 55–56
Christian educators, definition of, 56
Classism, 16–17, 77, 91, 133
Clergy, 69, 78–80, 101, 138–39; as learners, 133; as teachers, 129–31, 138–39
Communion, 144–46

Community, 66–68, 120–21
Congregations, 70, 129, 130, 136–37, 138, 140, 143–44
Conscientization, 46–48
Contextualism, 37–38
Contextualization, 37–38, 89–91
Conversion, 18, 68, 70–71, 72, 74–75; biblical foundation of, 56–60; definition of, 56–57, 59–60, 74–75; as principle of Christian education, 60–63
Cook, Guillermo, 3, 9, 26, 89
Costa Rica, x, xiii–xvi, xxiv–xxv, 69
Costas, Orlando, xxvi, 9, 16, 59, 74, 82, 147, 156
Cremin, Lawrence A., 111, 112
Crossing over, xviii
Curriculum, 112, 129, 137, 138–41

Destroyers of life, 2–7
Doubt, 139

Ecclesiology, 10
Ecuador, xvi–xxi, 16, 91

Ecumenical dialogue, xvii, xxviii, xxxi, 10, 12, 23–24
Education: as banking, 44; content of, 43–46, 88, 139–40; context of, 34, 39–40, 89–91; definition of, 28, 61, 85, 101; method of, 46–48; multicultural models of, 112–19; paradigms of, 84–88, 102–5; persons in, 89; process of, 139; purposes of, 30–31, 38–40, 140–41; reconstructionist philosophy of, 34–36, 47; theological foundation of, 30–34; in the United States, 110–12
Educational trinity, 28, 30, 40, 48, 61–62, 85–91
Eisner, Elliot W., 156
Elizondo, Virgilio, 107–8
ESEPA, xxviii, 94–95, 97–98
Ethnicity, xvii, 4, 17, 108–10, 118–19
Eucharist, 145–46
Exile, 123–27
Ezra, 129–31; book of, 123–25

Fackre, Gabriel, 78, 83, 101
Family: general, xi, 4, 6; personal, xvi–xvii, xxiii–xxiv, xxv, 106; value of, 120–21
Fiesta, 73, 122
Five-task model, 28, 36, 62–63, 64
Foulkes, Irene W., 7
Foundational Issues in Christian Education (Pazmiño), 153, 154
Fragmentation, 63–64, 83
Freire, Paulo: affirmation of, 51–52; as critic, prophet, 34–35; life of, 29–30; pedagogy of,

34–36, 41–43, 45–48; reappraisal of, 49–52; theology of, 49–50; three views of religion, 32–34

Galilee, 108–9
Globalization, 10, 40, 64, 100
God, as teacher, 81, 128–29, 134–36
González, Justo L., 121, 147
Gutierrez, Gustavo, 3, 8–9

Heschel, Abraham, 14
Hinojosa, Francisco Gomez, 100–101
Hispanic culture, 119–22
Humanism, humanization, 18, 29
Human rights, xxi, 4, 72

Identity, xxix
Ideology, 5, 84
Incarnation, 18, 37

Jesus, xi–xii, xxii, 9, 57, 65, 118, 124, 131, 134
Johnson, Susanne, 138
Journey, xi–xii, xxv–xxvi, xxix, xxx
Justice, xxi, 14–15, 71–73

La Belle, Thomas J., 84–85
Laity, 69, 76–83, 100–101, 103–5, 137; as learners, 133–34, 137; as teachers, 131–32, 137–38
Land, 15
Latin America, 1–2, 10–11, 65, 67, 69, 71–72, 73, 76–77, 82–85, 124, 142–43

Latin American Biblical Seminary (SBL), x, xxvi, xxviii, 7, 91–94, 97–98
Learners, 133
Levites, 131–32
Liberation: as content of education, 43–46; levels of, 8–10; theology of, 1, 9–10, 18–20, 25–27
Little, Sara, 30
López, Felicísimo, xviii–xxi

Mañana, 121–22
Marxism, 20, 22–25, 29, 51
Mission, 9–10, 64, 79, 101, 102, 135, 136, 140–41, 146
Multicultural education, 84, 100, 103–4, 117–19

Neal, Marie Augusta, 36
Nehemiah, 125–26, 141–43; book of, 125–27
Nicaragua, xxi–xxiii, 69, 90
Niebuhr, Hulda, 138
North America, and interaction with South America, xii–xiii, 10–12, 18–22
North American Hispanics, 1, 12, 24, 106–11, 119–22, 124, 146

Orthodoxy, 11, 24, 44, 62–63, 109
Orthopathos, 24, 62–63
Orthopraxis, 11, 24, 44–45, 62–63
Osmer, Richard R., 123, 136

Partnership, 78–79, 83, 127–35
Passion, 120
Pastor. See Clergy
Paulston, Rolland G., 84–87

Philemon, book of, 17–18, 66
Poverty, xiv–xvi, xxii, 3–4, 13, 20, 63–64, 67, 70, 93, 133, 142–43
Praxis, 24, 31, 41, 42–45, 102
Principles and Practices of Christian Education (Pazmiño), 28, 155
Problem-posing pedagogy, 42, 88–89, 96, 98, 141
Problems: ecological, xv, 5–6, 15; ecclesiastical, xxi, xxvii–xxviii, 7, 92, 93; economic, xiv–xvi, xvii; educational, xx–xxi, 141–44; health, 6; political, xiv–xvi, xviii–xx, xxii–xxiii
Proclamation, 64–65, 120
Program development, 138–41
PSI, 95–98

Reformation, 76–78, 132
Righteousness, 14–15

Sawicki, Marianne, 153
SBL. See Latin American Biblical Seminary
Schipani, Daniel S., 50, 52
Service, 68–71, 121
Sin, 19, 133
Soelle, Dorothee, 21–22
Solidarity, 13–15, 67
Solivan, Samuel, 24, 44, 62
Suffering, xxii, 12, 17–22, 67; church's response to, 7–10, 67; three phases of, 21–22

Teachers, 128–32
Theological education, xxvii, 36, 38–40, 44–48, 53–54, 80, 82–91, 137; alternative forms, 53,

Theological education (*cont.*)
91–98, 102–5; by extension,
77–78, 98–99
Theology: doing theology, 44–45;
related to education, 30–34
Transformation, 8, 24, 36, 67,
72, 74–75, 123; definition of,
55–56

United States, 11, 16, 63–64, 69,
71, 91, 99, 110–12

Villafañe, Eldin, 156
Violence, 4–5

Women, 4–5, 6, 20–21, 67–68
Work, 121, 142
Worship, 73–74, 122, 133,
144–46

Xenocentrism, 40, 154

Yoder, John H., 124